# Mystics of Islam

ADEPTS IN THE EASTERN
ESOTERIC TRADITION, PART 4

MANLY P. HALL

# MYSTICS OF ISLAM

Copyright © 1983 by the Philosophical Research Society, Inc.
2009 EDITION

All Rights Reserved. This book or parts thereof, may not be reproduced in any form without written permission from the publisher.

**ISBN-10 | 0-89314-532-7**
**ISBN-13 | 978-0-89314-532-3**

Cover Art: *detail of an illuminated manuscript of portions of "The Koran" in Arabic (17th Century) from the PRS Library Collection.*

Cover Layout and Design for this Edition: *Paul K. Austad*

Printed in the United States of America

---

Published by

THE PHILOSOPHICAL RESEARCH SOCIETY
3910 Los Feliz Boulevard
Los Angeles, CA 90027 USA

*phone* | 323.663.2167
*fax* | 323.663.9443
*website* | www.prs.org
*general inquiries* | info@prs.org
*mail order* | mailorder@prs.org

# THE MYSTICS OF ISLAM

### Introduction

The purpose of the present work is to point out the original existence and present survival of an Adept tradition in the Moslem world. We must therefore demonstrate that such a belief was anciently held among these people, and also that it has survived in modern times as a mystical or secret conviction. There can be no doubt that the belief in Adept and Initiate teachers and mystical sages possessing supernatural powers is the "mind" of Islam, though not actually canonical. Devout believers were not criticized nor rebuked for holding such opinions. The Moslem world has always acknowledged the importance of mysticism and bestowed the highest approbation upon its poets, visionaries, and metaphysical thinkers. In conformity with world custom, it has also invested its saints with legends, and ascribed miracles to them. It has also acknowledged the existence of esoteric disciplines for the unfoldment of the potential spiritual resources of the human being.

Moslem scholars have frequently implied in their writings that secret schools arose early in the unfoldment of the Moslem faith. Some of these were founded by philosophers and scientists. Others, however, seem to have originated among mystics for the peculiar purpose of perpetuating the inner meaning of the Moslem faith. The principal arcana of these colleges or assemblages were concerned with systems of meditation, concentration, and Yogic practices similar to those of Hindu mystics. Such spiritual exercises resulted in the development of internal faculties and the ability to control natural phenomena. Writers have noted that the teachings of the secret Moslem sects also derived important philosophical and theurgic elements from Gnosticism, Neoplatonism, Judaism and Christianity.

In the light of a gradually increasing insight into the Moslem esoteric tradition, it becomes easier to relate the beliefs of these people to the universal pattern of comparative mysticism. What may at first seem to be a fanciful and extravagant literature, reveals an important philosophical system to those who are willing to recognize mysticism *per se* as a rational approach to the mysteries of life. It becomes apparent that the religion founded by Mohammed was always divisible into two clearly defined streams of tradition, one esoteric, and the other, exoteric. As in Greek philosophy, the esoteric part was intentionally concealed, and its true keys were transmitted orally. There are, however, broad hints and intimations to be found in the writings of initiated scholars. These men, faithful to their obligations of secrecy, have followed the traditional procedure. They have concealed their deeper secrets under elaborate symbolical devices completely meaningless to the uninitiated.

Jaffur Shurreef describes the rituals used by the Moslems of India in initiating a devotee. He writes: "The *Moorshud* then reveals to the disciple, in a whisper, (lit. breast to breast, hand in hand, and lip to ear), all the secret mysteries of godliness."* The reference here to the ritual of Blue Lodge Masonry has been noted by a number of Masonic writers. In his *Indian Masons' Marks of the Mogul Dynasty,* A. Gorham concludes that guilds of operative Masons were employed by the Mogul emperors from the time of Akbar to the decline of the empire. He assumes, therefore, that guilds of builders, with their usual philosophical objectives flourished in this region, preserving the old mystery religion as perpetuated by various groups since the time of the Dionysian Artificers of Greece. The masters of these guilds and their qualified workmen marked the

---

* Qanoon-E-Islam.

stones of the great Moslem monuments with distinguishing symbols, as was later the practice of the Cathedral Builders of Europe.

The contact between Islam and Christendom during and immediately following the tragic cycle of the Crusades, resulted in the introduction of Islamic philosophy among European peoples. Paracelsus visited Constantinople, where he discovered that the Moslem physicians were far more advanced in the diagnosis and treatment of disease than the European doctors. The early alchemists, including Roger Bacon and Basil Valentin, began to refer to the Arabs as masters of the alchemistical philosophy. Geber and Avicenna are referred to as "Adepts of the Stone," and numerous truth-seekers journeyed to the Near East and North Africa to study with famous Masters of the Law of Islam. There seems to have been comparatively little prejudice among these savants, and they returned in due time to their European homes with extraordinary reports of the wisdom and liberality they had encountered in the schools and universities of Cairo, Baghdad, and Damascus.

Moslem mysticism may be regarded as a heritage of spiritual insight, served and perpetuated by a minority group among the followers of the Prophet Mohammed. Edward William Lane-Poole in notes to his translation of the *Arabian Nights Entertainment,* discusses the lives and miracles of Moslem saints. He embellishes his account with stories of their miracles and other remarkable evidences of their sanctity. He writes, "The distinguished individuals (saints) above mentioned are known by the common appelation of 'Welees' or particular favorites of God. The more eminent among them composed a mysterious hierarchical body, whose government respects the whole human race, infidels as well as believers; but whose power is often exercised in such a manner that the subjects influenced by it know not from what person or persons its effects proceed . . . . Their supernatural powers they are supposed to obtain by right of the most exalted piety, and especially by constant self-denial, accompanied with the most implicit reliance upon God; by the services of good genii; and, as many believe, by the knowledge and utterance of 'the most great name' of God."

This classic statement is applicable to all systems teaching the existence of Adept or Initiate sages. It is by a scholar who devoted the greater part of his life to the study of the religion, philosophy, and literature of Islam. He lived for a great many years among Moslems and was sympathetic to their ideas and doctrines. His words leave no doubt that these people were not only aware of the doctrine of Adepts, but embraced it as an essential part of their basic concept of the operation of the Divine Power in the material world.

MANLY P. HALL

Los Angeles, California
1975

# THE ADEPTS

## THE MYSTICS OF ISLAM

*"In the name of God, the Compassionate, the Merciful."\**
(The Koran)

The prevailing spirit of Mediterranean Christianity during the 5th and 6th Centuries A.D. resulted in the relentless persecution of non-conformists within the faith itself and those pagans who declined to become converts. To escape danger and embarrassment, Grecian teachers, together with the leaders and members of heretical Christian groups, sought refuge outside the temporal jurisdiction of the rising and expanding Church. Many of these scholars, including Jewish and Syrian mystics, found the Arabian atmosphere congenial to study and meditation. They were honorably received, and their doctrines were tolerantly examined. This spirit of temperance toward learning resulted in the assembling of a brilliant constellation of learned men, who contributed powerfully to the glory of Baghdad, Alexandria, and other Moslem cities.

The temperate atmosphere of Arabian culture, however, also led to disastrous complications. Fanatics of every degree also found asylum in the towns and villages of the desert. Most of these extremists had suffered in their own lands, and to their basic intensities were added psychological pressures and powerful personal animosities. Gradually, the dignity of Near Eastern living was seriously disturbed. Dermenghem summarizes the spiritual confusion among the Arab people which undoubtedly inspired Mohammed—

---

\* Every section of the Koran, except one, begins with these words.

a sincere and naturally devout man—to instigate a sweeping program of theological reform. "Arabia was the meeting-place of heresies, *haeresium ferax,*" said one of the Fathers in the Fifth Century. It would not have been easy to know where one stood amongst the Sabellians, the Docetes who denied Christ's human existence (regarding his body as a phantom), the Arians who denied his divinity, the Eutycheans, the Jacobites and the Monophysites who denied his double nature, the Nestorians who saw in him two persons, the Mariamites and the Collyridians who worshiped Mary, the Antidicomariamites who denied her perpetual virginity, the Judeo-Christian Nazarites and Ebionites, the anti-Jewish Marcionites, Gnostics, the Valentinians, the Basilidians, the Carpocratians, the Rakusians, etc.... There is an Abyssinian proverb which says that the Christians never agree except on one point: the birth of Christ.\*

The region in which the faith of Islam had its origin was by no means an untutored or uncultured area. The people apparently belonged to the Semitic family, and the land was supposed to have been the allotment of Shem, the son of Noah. The inhabitants are physically a splendid type, distinguished for their clean, simple abstemious habits; and the illnesses of Western civilization are almost unknown among them. This is pointed out by D. F. Warin, who visited the area at the time of the conflict between King Hussein and the Wahhabis under the leadership of Ibn Saud, Sultan of Nejd (1916-1924). At an earlier date, Sir William Willcocks, Consulting Engineer to the Turkish government in Mesopotamia, had this to say of the happy state of affairs enjoyed by the natives of Arabistan: "Long may the Arabs keep to their simple and natural life in their native deserts and conserve a type of manhood and womanhood which does credit to the world. Few people could say as I have heard these people say, that they know of no illness except the illness of death."†

---

\* Emile Dermenghem, *The Life of Mahomet.*
† *From the Garden of Eden to the Crossing of the Jordan.*

If these people are so naturally fortunate, they are subject also to certain misfortunes. Their way of life has long been burdened with problems of physical survival. These people are agriculturists and sheepherders, and the need for water has brought these ancient vocations into dramatic conflict as typified by the tragedy of Cain and Abel. The wise men of the desert say that if water for the land and the sheep could be assured, the brotherhood of man could come to the Hejaz. Government has also rested heavily upon these Arabs, even though rulership has seldom been tyrannical or oppressive. The citizens simply grow weary of leaders, good or bad, and most administrations are short-lived.

The pious Moslem assumes that the centuries which preceded the birth of the Prophet were times of benightedness and ignorance. However, as has already been noted, this is not strictly true, except in the sense that a strong central spiritual leadership was lacking. It is noted that in earlier days, writing and poetry were encouraged as fine arts, eloquence was particularly admired, and annual assemblies and contests were held, devoted to skill in poetry and oratory. Religion consisted of the worship of heavenly bodies, and most uncomplicated idolatry. Arabia was not an uncultured region at the time of the birth of the Prophet, but actually heavy-laden with philosophic speculations. Dermenghem paints an interesting picture of the intellectual environment in which the faith of Mohammed arose.

"Every corner of the town," said a Father of the Church, "is filled with discussion: markets, clothing-stalls, money-changers and provision-dealers. Do you want to change a gold-piece? They begin to philosophize upon what is begotten and what is not begotten. Do you want to know the price of bread? They reply: 'The Father is greater than the Son.' Do you ask if your bath is hot? The attendant tells you: 'The Son was created out of nothingness.' "*

---

* Dermenghem, *op. cit.*

It is evident that Arabia received into itself the doctrines and beliefs of many peoples. At least several of the sects known to have flourished there practiced philosophical disciplines, formed secret schools and colleges, gathered disciples, initiated their advanced students, and actually claimed to participate in the Adept Tradition. This is not only clear from the historical orientation, but is proved by the later rise of mystical speculations among the Moslems themselves. They reveal their indebtedness to the same essential sources of knowledge that enriched Greece, Egypt, and the Valley of the Euphrates.

It was not against the democracy of true learning that Mohammed introduced his faith. He undoubtedly experienced in himself the need for a simple and direct religion that would relieve the faithful of the burden of distracting uncertainties. That such was actually the case may be gathered from a statement made by Mohammed's first cousin, Ja'far ben Abi Talib, to the Negus of Ethiopia. He told this great sovereign that the people of Arabia were in the shadow of a strange kind of ignorance, worshiping idols and conducting themselves according to the concept of the survival of the fittest. In this emergency, God, the Compassionate, the Merciful, established among them a man of their own race who commanded them to worship one God, cast out superstition, shun vice, practice virtue, and in all things to be sincere, devout, charitable and chaste. He caused them also to recognize the dignity of prayer, the goodness of sharing with the needy, and the self-discipline of fasting. Because this man was good, and practiced his goodness in his own life, his people accepted him and believed in his mission.

## *Mohammed, Prophet of Islam*

That part of Arabia Felix which is known as the Hejaz, a province extending along the coast of the Red Sea from the Gulf of Akaba to Taif, may properly be called the Holy

The Great Mosque at Mecca with the Kaaba in the center. From an Indian Print.

Land of Islam. Within the boundaries of this region are the two sacred cities, Mecca the Honored, the birthplace of the Prophet; and Medina the Good, where Mohammed died. In this area of strange contrasts of arid deserts and flowering gardens, one of the great religions of the world came into being, and from this humble and distant land, it extended its authority to many nations and the most remote parts of the world. Today the faith of Islam numbers nearly four hundred seventy-five million beings. Five time a day the faithful face Mecca and give thanks for the spiritual convictions which have descended to them from the pages of the Glorious Koran.

A man walking the streets of Mecca in the early years of the Seventh Century A.D., might have noticed a quiet and thoughtful Arab of middle life, a mantle across his shoulders and his head-scarf drawn over his face. In his book, *The Procession of the Gods,* G. G. Atkins gives an impression of this dignified Arabian, who was to change the history of the whole world. "Mohammed was spare in figure, above middle size, well boned and broad-chested. His head was unusually large, his forehead broad and commanding. He had large, black, searching eyes under arched and meeting eyebrows, an aquiline nose, good teeth, well apart. His expression was pensive and contemplative, his beard . . . was thick and black. He walked quickly as though he were going uphill. He was of winning manners, generally silent in company; but when he spoke, it was to the point." Upon this citizen of Mecca, prominent both by birth and by marriage, was to descend the wrath and hatred of many associates who now cultivated his acquaintance.

It is inevitable that there would be two divergent accounts of the birth and early life of Mohammed. The first and natural account set forth simple facts, which were commonplace, and, to a large measure the account which the Prophet himself preferred. He used every possible means to prevent himself from being considered glamorous. He performed no miracles, claimed no supernatural powers, and insisted that, like all other men, he was subject to infirmities of mind, soul, and body. He desired to be respected for one virtue alone: sincerity of purpose. The second and more glorified account originated among the tents in the desert, where men gathered in the dark evenings under stars and vied with each other in the art of storytelling. Their fabrications were not merely contests of oratory; they were the homage of the Arab paying tribute in his own way to the admiration, veneration, and even awe in which he held the person, the life, and the teaching of the founder of his faith. The popular account of the Prophet's life can logically be introduced by the familiar line, "Once upon a time . . ."

In the twenty-fifth year of his age, Abdallah, whose name means "the servant of God," was affianced by his father to Amina, the beautiful, virtuous and lovable daughter of Wahb. Abdallah must have been the most prepossessing of all young men, for it is reported—and who shall deny the story—that on the day of his marriage to Amina, two hundred damsels of Mecca died of broken hearts. Not long after his marriage, Abdallah, bidding his bride, Amina, an affectionate farewell, departed on a mercantile expedition which led him into the southern part of Syria. After successfully completing his business, he hastened to return to his wife but was taken sick at Medina and died shortly after, leaving a heritage of five camels, a herd of goats, and a faithful slave girl.

Due to the lack of reliable biographical information available in English, there is some question as to whether Mohammed was born prior to or after his father's death. However, the most approved tradition among the faithful, states that he was a "widow's son." Even if the story has been changed to contrive this circumstance, it would indicate an effort to make the birth conform with an ancient mystical tradition. Among peoples where the concept of the "widow's son" had general acceptance, this term implied a prophet or an initiate of sacred rites and mysteries, or an adept of the secret doctrine.

Mohammed, Prophet of Islam, upon whose name be peace, was born between A.D. 570 and 572. Some historians, including Moslems, favor April 20, 571 A.D., as the most authentic date. Again legend embellishes intervals of historical silence. Accounts usually associated with the birth of a divine or sanctified person are present, and many marvels are duly recorded. It is said that the Prophet existed before the creation of the world, and that, had it not been for him, the sun and the moon and the stars would never have been created. He was fashioned out of the light of God, but it was also affirmed that this statement applied to his spiritual essence rather than to his physical body. It was predestined and foreordained that Mohammed's birthplace should be Mecca, that he should migrate to Medina, that his name should be Mohammed, and that he should never utter an untruth.

The mother of the Prophet, upon whose name be honor, related that immediately prior to his birth, a terrible sound filled the atmosphere. While she was trembling with fear, a white bird came out of the invisible laying its wing upon her breast, and filling her heart with peace and serenity. According to the storytellers, many frightening occurrences accompanied the nativity of the Prophet. Lake Sawa flowed back into its secret fountains; the River Tigris burst its bounds; the palace of the King of Persia shook, and its towers fell; all the idols of the world were overthrown; and a great light came from the sky, filling the hearts of men with hope and gratitude.

When she gave birth to her babe, the widowed Amina was refreshed by a wonderful beverage in a jeweled cup presented to her by an unseen hand. Voices were heard in the house, and although there were sounds of footsteps and the rustle of garments, no person was to be seen. Were not these invisible beings the saints of old times, the prophets, and the patriarchs who had come to witness the predestined event? A veil let down from the sky covered Amina, hiding the birth from mortal view. Strange birds with beaks of ruby and wings of emerald strutted about singing beautiful songs.

The moment the child was born, he prostrated himself on the ground and, raising his hands, prayed earnestly for the forgiveness of his people. His aunt, Safia, recorded that Mohammed was born circumcised, and that a few moments after his birth, he recited the creed. The seal of prophecy was upon his body in letters of light. Also at this time, three persons, surrounded by a brilliance like the sun, appeared from heaven. One held a silver goblet; another, an emerald tray; and the third, a silken towel. These heavenly visitors bathed Mohammed seven times and then saluted him as the "Prince of Mankind." In the midst of these other wonders, a glorious light surrounded the house, and this light seemed to emanate from the body of Amina. So brilliant was this lumination that it was visible from a great distance. Amina reported that she felt no discomfort at the birth of her child, and that a messenger had come to her from the sky before her son was born. This messenger told her that she had been elected to be the mother of the Prophet, who was to be the Lord of his people. The messenger told her that she was to call her child Ahmed (Praised), and that he was to be the Desired of All Nations. Through him, the original faith of the world would be restored to mankind.

As soon as her child was born, Amina, according to the fashion of her people, sent a messenger with the good tidings to Abd al Muttalib, the father of her late husband. When the news reached him, this venerable man was seated within the sacred court of the Kaaba in the midst of his sons and the principal men of his tribe. The old man rejoiced greatly, and went immediately to Amina, who narrated to him all the miracles that had occurred. Then Abd al Muttalib took the child in his arms and went to the Kaaba and, standing beside the Holy House before the Aerolite of Abraham, gave thanks to God. It is written that at that time, the name Mohammed was bestowed upon the child.

According to Katib al Wackidi, a miraculous circumstance took place when Mohammed was a child of three or four years. He was playing one morning with his foster brother and sister near the encampment of his people when suddenly two angels appeared. One of them, presumably Gabriel, opened the body of the little boy, took out his heart, and cleansed from it the black drops of original sin which all mortals have inherited from their forefather, Adam. The angels then washed the inside of the boy's body with water of snow held in a golden platter. They then weighted his body against a thousand of his people, and he outweighed them all. The angels then returned the heart to its proper place, and the body of the Prophet became luminous. He seemed to shine with a mysterious radiance like that which has flowed from all of God's messengers, according to the records of ancient times. Many who could not actually see this light experienced it in their souls so that they were drawn to Mohammed and believed in him.

These accounts are not more extravagant than the legends which have accumulated around the founders of most religions. It is fully evident that the followers of Mohammed accepted him as a messenger sent from God, bearing the Divine authority and destined for his ministry. The birth stories parallel in many ways the accounts circulated about the nativities of Buddha, Confucius, and Jesus. Although the tendency has been to dismiss these tales as pious inventions, the psychological aspects of such archetypal legends are now being given greater consideration. There is a reason for everything in this world, and the definite effort of Moslem mystics and philosophers to bring the story of Mohammed's advent and nativity into line with the mystical tradition is neither accidental nor fortuitous. Under the surface of fantasy is a firm symbolical structure unchanging since the dawn of time.

Because of the numerous sects which have arisen in the Moslem world, it is difficult to speak in a way broadly representative of current opinion. It is certain, however, that the

Prophet has become a personification of holiness and the path by which it is attained. The Prophet personifies a degree of consciousness which, when born within man, is attended by wonders. In him ancient beliefs, like the towers of Persia, are shaken down, materialistic instincts are troubled, fountains of false inspiration become dry at their sources; and the directions of revelation are reversed. The chalice of ecstasy sustains the soul of the mystic through his ordeal. Trances and visions are accorded to him. He is born again to become one with the Prophet, who stands as an embodiment of the Messianic Dispensation. This becomes more evident when the doctrines of the Dervishes and the Sufis are examined.

It was the custom of the Arabs of that day to appoint a nurse for a newborn infant, and Mohammed was given into the care of Halima, belonging to the tribe of Banu Sa't. He stayed with her until his sixth year, and was then returned to his mother. Shortly after this, Amina resolved to make a journey to the tomb of her husband at Medina. Mohammed traveled with her, and during this journey his mother died. Although the father of the Prophet had many brothers, it was Abd al Muttalib, the grandfather, who assumed the guardianship. When Mohammed was eight, however, his noble grandfather died, and Abu Talib, the paternal uncle, took the lad into his house and heart. Mohammed developed the deepest affection for Abu Talib and was his constant companion. The various people with whom he was intimately associated in early life formed the Assembly of the Companions, and their words and opinions were second in authority only to the precepts of the Koran.

When Mohammed was about twelve years of age, it is believed that he accompanied his uncle, Abu Talib, on a caravan journeying to Syria. In due course, they arrived at Basra, which lay beyond the Jordan and was the country of the tribe of Manassah. At that time, there was a strong settlement of Nestorian Christians at Basra, and the caravan of Abu Talib encamped near a community of Nestorian monks. Here the travelers were entertained with all hospitality. One or two of the monks conversed with Mohammed on this occasion, and were deeply impressed by the precocity of his mind and his eager desire for information on matters of religion. It has been assumed that the doctrines he learned from these Christian monks turned Mohammed against idolatry. The Nestorians were so opposed to worshiping images of any kind that they seldom displayed even the cross, although it was then a general emblem of Christianity. In later visits to Syria, Mohammed continued his interest in the teachings of the Christian community. When he was about twenty-five years of age, and once more in Basra, he is said to have had an interview with Nestorius, who embraced him as the coming prophet. As the founder of the Nestorian sect died in the Fifth Century, Mohammed must have met a later monk of the same name.

Critical study has caused some doubt as to the source of Mohammed's knowledge or opinions about Christianity. References in the Koran do not seem to emphasize the Nestorian concepts, although the Prophet appears to have had special respect for certain communities of priests and monks, as indicated in the Koran by Sura V:91. It is also believed that, had Mohammed been deeply versed in Nestorianism, he would have specifically referred to it in the Koran, for direct reference was his common practice. Certain it is, however, that as a young man, he was seriously disillusioned with such available information about the general state of Christendom as he was able to acquire. There is much to indicate that he might have accepted Judaism or Christianity as his own religion rather than founding a new sect. The pressures of bickering and controversy of the early Church impelled him to seek the original and pure religion of the prophets and patriarchs, which he felt had fallen into evil times. Moslemism is firmly established in the conviction that there is no God but God. Because Deity is one and alone and there can be no other God besides Him,

Mohammed could not accept the divinity of Jesus or the doctrine of the Holy Trinity. He was willing to acknowledge Jesus as a holy prophet whose teachings were true, but not believe the dogma that the Nazarene Master was coidentical and consubstantial with God, the Father. He also clearly stated that he regarded himself as merely a human being, and the entire example of his life proves conclusively that he was not depreciating the spiritual attainments of others in any effort to advance his own reputation. He forbade the deification of his own name or memory, affirming of his life that there was "no God but God."

In various periods of the world's history, God, in his infinite wisdom, caused prophets to rise up and bear witness to the pure revelation of spiritual truth. Of such were the great teachers described in the Old Testament, and likewise Jesus. Mohammed went so far as to say that his own coming was prophesied in the Old Testament, and also that after him, another teacher would appear who was to be "the Desired of All Nations." Christian scholars have liked to affirm that Mohammed had a very slight and superficial knowledge of Christianity, and that his opinions, therefore, were based mainly on hearsay. This may be questioned, however, for it is known that members of his own family had been converted to Christianity, as it then existed in that region. The truth probably is that the Christian communities in Arabia were themselves comparatively uninformed, and that their beliefs were uncertain and conflicting and therefore not suitable to advance a solid knowledge of the faith.

Abu Talib, the esteemed uncle of the Prophet, is authority for the statement that during his entire youth, Mohammed never quarreled with anyone. When he was about twenty years old, he joined a society known as the *Hilful-Fuzul*, the members of which had taken a solemn oath to help the needy and the poor, safeguard the rights of the oppressed, and support the cause of justice.

When he was about twenty-six years of age, Mohammed

was manager of the estate of a wealthy widow named Khadijah. She so admired his ability and his integrity that they were married, although she was fifteen years his senior. Six children were born of this union, but Fatima, the youngest of the daughters, alone survived her father, and she outlived him by only six months. By another alliance, made later in life, Mohammed also had a son named Ibrahim. This child also died in infancy.

After his marriage with Khadijah, Mohammed came under the influence of her cousin, Waraqua ibn Naufal, who was a man of philosophical attainments and esoteric interests. It is said that his insight was great, even though his body was feeble and long study had brought blindness to his eyes. Washington Irving says that he was "originally a Jew, subsequently a Christian, and withal a pretender to astrology." * The word *pretender*, in this case, probably reflects only Washington Irving's skepticism about astrology. In the days of the Prophet, this science was highly reputable, and followers thereof were usually men of mystical attainments and philosophical distinction. Waraqua ibn Naufal is mentioned as the first to translate sections of the Old and New Testaments into Arabic. Seeking for some rational explanation for Mohammed's acquaintance with the *Mishnah*, the *Talmud*, and related works, his wife's cousin looms large as a possibility. The wise Waraqua may well have strongly influenced the mind of Mohammed. It is said that Waraqua was waiting for the advent of the promised prophet, and he supported Mohammed's claim to his ministry.

There are many ways in which a thoughtful man can come under strong religious influence. The Roman governor of Egypt sent to Mohammed a Christian slave girl, who is remembered as Mary the Copt. She became the mother of the Prophet's son Ibrahim, and this in itself should indicate that Mohammed was free of all unreasonable prejudice against the Christian sect. It is interesting to speculate upon

---

* See *Mahomet and His Successors.*

the possibilities, had Ibrahim lived to establish the descent of the House of the Prophet. Coptic Christianity, therefore, came into the home of Mohammed, and its teachings, at least in a simple form most agreeable with his own thinking, were readily available.

It is generally assumed that up to his fortieth year, Mohammed was a devout and sincere follower of the beliefs of ancient Arabia. He seems to have differed from the people around him mainly because of his mystical inclinations and strong imaginative powers. He customarily spent the month of Ramadan on Mount Hira, living in a cave and performing ascetic exercises. This form of retreat included nights devoted to prayer, a period of fasting, and the bestowal of gifts upon the poor. When he returned to Mecca, Mohammed would then walk seven times around the Kaaba before returning to his own house.

It was during the rites of Ramadan that Mohammed began to question the integrity and sufficiency of the prevailing religion. Some say that while on Mount Hira he met an eccentric mystic who induced him to consider more seriously the elements of Jewish and Christian beliefs. As confusion and uncertainty increased within him, Mohammed returned more frequently to Mount Hira. Sacrificing many of the practical concerns of living, he became a recluse, returning home only to secure the necessities of existence. Accounts indicate that he passed through metaphysical experiences similar to those described in the lives of many mystics, including mystical experiences as described by St. John of the Cross in his book *The Dark Night of the Soul*.

It was in the cave on Mount Hira, now known as the Mountain of Light, that a vision or superphysical occurrence took place. Mohammed beheld an angelic figure surrounded by light, holding in its hands a silken shawl or scarf with mysterious characters traced upon it. Holding out the scarf toward Mohammed, the angel said to him, "Read." There is some uncertainty as to the meaning of the answer given by Mohammed. Some versions state that he could not read; and others, that he did not wish to read. In the end, the angel read to him the verses written upon the scarf. On this same occasion, the angel, said to be Gabriel, declared Mohammed to be the true prophet of the living God.

After the mystical experiences, Mohammed hastened home and described the occurrence to his wife Khadijah. He was confused and alarmed lest some evil spirit of the old pagan faith was attempting to deceive him.

The deep change that came about in Mohammed's personality was interpreted in various ways by his friends, rivals, and later, by the orthodox members of the prevailing religion. A few regarded him as inspired; some as a *kahin,* or soothsayer; many believed him to suffer from hallucinations; and at least a few forthrightly considered him insane or under the supernatural influence of Satan and his minions. According to Khadijah, he shared most of the negative opinions of himself, and frequently asked if he was possessed by *jinn,* or malicious sprites. Khadijah was a constant source of courage and inspiration. She reminded her husband that he had always been a good and honorable man, that his motives were honest and devout, and there was no reason to assume that the powers of evil would have any authority over his conduct. Khadijah seems to have sensed his destiny, for it is recorded that she said to him, "Thou wilt be the Prophet of thy nation."

To give him further faith and assurance, Khadijah took Mohammed to her cousin Waraqua, whose wisdom was widely respected. Waraqua verified that Mohammed had been given the great *nomos,* the law which is like the *nomos* of Moses. The term *nomos* is from the Greek, and seems to signify a spirit or a being who knows the most secret thoughts of man. Also spelled *namus,* it is the law, a communicator of secret messages, an institute or a power, a transcendent means by which things are accomplished according to the Divine Will. It has been associated with the word *Torah,* as the revealed law of the Jews.

Waraqua declared that the vision which had come to Mohammed indicated that he was destined for a great mission among his people, and that he, Waraqua, believed fully in him, and desired to assist him but regretted that he would not be alive when the day of destiny came. Khadijah also went to a monk known as Addas, who confirmed the words of Waraqua, and this support of those near to him and wise in such mysteries was of the greatest consolation to Mohammed. Khadijah, upon her let the grace of Allah rest, was the first of his house to embrace the doctrine and is referred to as the first Moslem woman and the mother of the believers.

It is recorded that Mohammed was seven years in preparation for his ministry. His long vigils had not only impaired his health, but had brought about fainting spells, which the Moslem mystics considered to be ecstatic trances. Similar occurrences are also reported of Dante and St. Francis of Assisi. Most of the Suras, or sections, of the Koran were written while the Prophet was in this trance-like condition. These attacks often came without warning. In some cases Mohammed would fall unconscious, and at other times he would sit wrapped in blankets with cold sweat pouring from his face and body, even on the hottest days. While in this strange condition, he would speak, and his words were either written down, or else memorized by his small circle of devoted friends. It was in this way that a considerable part of the Koran was written. Later in life, Mohammed said to Abu Bakr that every white hair in his beard was a Sura of the Koran.

## *The Glorious Koran*

The word *Koran,* (Arabic *Qur'an*), literally means *recitation,* and indicates the method by which the Suras, or sections, of the book were revealed to the Prophet. *Islam* is translated *submission,* and the religion, therefore, pro-

Page of a miniature Koran. This manuscript was written on Gazelle skin in Kufic characters by order of the Caliph Haroum al Rashid, in the year A.D. 798, and is reported to have been sent as a gift by the Caliph to the Emperor Charlemagne. From *Universal Palaeography* by M. J. B. Silvestre.

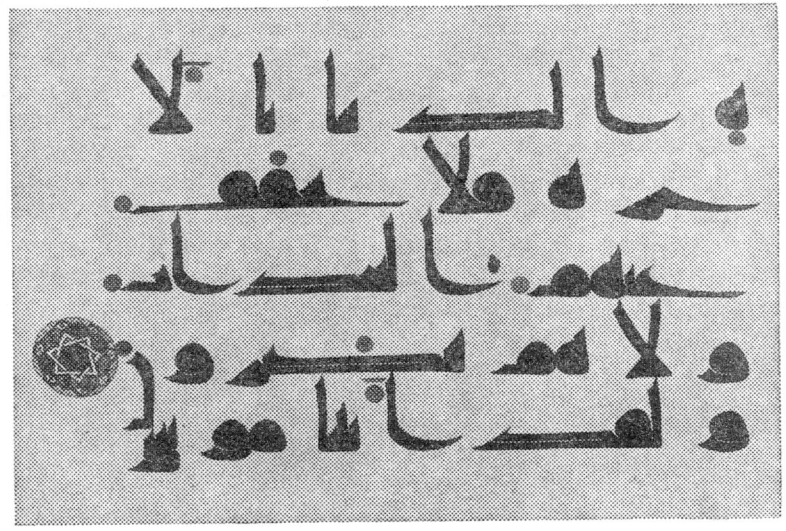

Leaf of a 7th Century Koran in Kufic writing. A finely executed specimen derived from Verse 80 of the Second Sura. Ornamented in gold and colors. From *Universal Palaeography* by M. J. B. Silvestre.

claims itself as a faith of submission to the Will of God. With a few clearly marked exceptions, the Koran is written in the first person, and the speaker is God. The book deals with a variety of subjects, including theology, ethics and jurisprudence. It has therefore become the foundation of the total Moslem life pattern. Idolatry and the deification of human beings are strictly forbidden. Such religious observances as fasting and pilgrimage are established and defined. The Moslem legal code is founded upon the authority of the Koran, and this brings the religion into direct contact with the private citizen and the concerns of his daily living.

In its structure, the Koran is similar to many other sacred books, but as always, there are certain differences which became increasingly important as the religion of Islam grew and spread. It is now held that all the sections of the Koran were actually dictated by the Prophet during his own lifetime. The arrangement of the Suras, however, is in some instances arbitrary, and resulted from learned councils by leaders of the faith. Substantially the book was compiled in the period between the Prophet's illumination and his death in A.D. 632, or A.H. 11, to use the Moslem method of recording.

The Koran parallels in many ways, the Old and New Testaments, and it must be assumed that Mohammed was not striving for originality. The work reveals a profound admiration of the life and ministry of Jesus. The moral codes and statutes of the Koran are heavily colored by the Mosaic law, and this followed into the priesthood, which held to the Jewish persuasion that the priest was essentially a teacher rather than an intermediary between God and man. In its present form, the Koran consists of one hundred and fourteen chapters, each of which has a title and a statement of the place in which it was revealed. Experts are of the opinion that the various sections reflect strongly the period of the Prophet's career during which the Suras were written. It is also a unique factor that certain verses were abrogated, that is, removed, or revoked, and other revelations put in their place. After the death of the Prophet, it appeared that some part of his instruction had not been committed to writing. The secretary of the Prophet, Zayd ibn Thabit, was entrusted with the sacred task of assembling all the sections and verses into one volume. For a time, apparently, only this one copy of the Koran existed. Later, this same Zayd was appointed to revise his previous compilation. This became the standard text, and most of the earlier manuscripts were destroyed. Thus there can be some doubt on particular aspects of the work, but as these revisions are early, they would not have been accepted had they deviated too widely from the popular tradition.

The Koran has been divided into four general institutes. The broad foundations of faith are associated with the earliest period of the revelation. Under the second heading are listed the procedures and forms of worship; under the third, the ethics or code of conduct; and under the fourth, the moral burden of the teaching, presented through legends, myths, fables, parables, and even historical incidents. The career of Mohammed, as revealed through the writings, is also divisible into three epochs. The first epoch reveals Mohammed as unfolding his own belief, and setting in motion the spiritual concept of his religion. In the second epoch, the faith takes on a more aggressive form and moves against the idolatrous systems and various other sects within the Moslem sphere of influence. In the third epoch Mohammed emerges as a ruler over his people, the Prince of the faithful, with both spiritual and temporal powers. His attitude becomes paternal, and the believers are regarded as his children. As necessary, he makes new laws, and revises those which had previously been given. Some have said that the Koran is a sacred commonplace book, combining doctrine and diary. Mohammed does not seem to object to revealing the transitions in his own nature which are inevitable to the development of his message.*

---

* For additional material, see HORIZON, Vol. 13, No. 3 (Winter 1953), "The Story of the Koran" by Manly P. Hall.

## The Hegira

The household of the Prophet supplied the first converts to his faith, and the circle rapidly increased to include a solid core of persons well known for their good moral character and respectability. After about four years of teaching privately to a group which had grown to exceed forty members, the Prophet was commanded by revelation to promulgate Islam publicly. Almost immediately his growing prestige caused fear and anxiety to the people of Mecca who profited greatly from the religion then prevailing in the city. They therefore decided to waive the ancient tradition that blood should not be spilled within the holy city and end the threat of Islam by assassinating the Prophet.

Mohammed, however, was given a revelation in the form of a warning, and God commanded him to take flight from Mecca or his life would be lost. This presented a rather difficult problem. The people of Mecca had so trusted the honesty of the Prophet that they had deposited their valuables in his house for protection. It was necessary to make arrangements to deliver all these belongings to their owners, and at the same time not reveal the intention of departing from the city. The Meccans surrounded the house of the Prophet, but the Angel of the Lord came in the night, and they fell asleep. In obedience to the Divine command, Mohammed came out of the house and, turning his eyes to the Kaaba, cried out, "O Mecca, thou hast been to me the dearest spot in all the world, but thy sons would not let me live."

Accompanied by Abu Bakr, the Prophet took refuge in the cave of Thawr, about three miles from Mecca. When the band of assassins discovered that Mohammed had escaped, they sent out parties to intercept his journey. One of these groups actually found the footsteps leading to the mouth of the cave. Then occurred the only miraculous circumstances said to be recorded in authentic Mussulman history. Emile Dermenghem gives a gracious description of the wonderful occurrences. "It was then that the miracle happened — a harmony of the soul of man and the outer world. In the arid crack of the rock, a mountain shrub had sprouted. It seemed suddenly to grow; its branches gripped the rocks; its graceful tendrils stood up in the air until almost all of the cave entrance was covered. In its shadow, a dove lay cooing, and a spider, performing its daily miracle, spread the intricate, geometrical pattern of its web. Between the light of the outside and the cool darkness of the cave extended the delicate threads at the end of which the spider balanced himself, climbed up, descended, and finally came to rest in the middle, lying in wait for his victim. And the white dove — the bird of love — laid her eggs in the sand. The male fluttered about her there at the entrance of the cave, their home. What joy on the earth, what love and peace in this tiny corner of the world! . . . The Qoraishites looked into the dark hole. They saw the dove but they did not want to crush her eggs. They saw the bush and the spider's web, and shook their heads, convinced that no one had entered the cave lately." *

On the fourth day, the Prophet and his party continued on his way to Medina, which they reached after a weary journey. In this city, Mohammed and Abu Bakr were given a warm reception, for the people were proud that the Prophet had decided to honor their community. The flight of Mohammed to Medina is called the *Hegira,* which literally means the *migration.* When capitalized, the word stands for the beginning of the Moslem era. It also distinguishes the circumstance of the departure of Mohammed from Mecca and, by extension, is applicable to the act of any Moslem leaving a country of another faith. Mystically, it is the moral act of fleeing from sin through dedication to the spiritual life. Various dates are given, differing, however, but slightly. It is said that Mohammed reached Medina on June 28,

---

* Dermenghem, *op. cit.*

# THE MYSTICS OF ISLAM

The Mosque at Medina where Mohammed began his ministry and where he died. From an Indian print.

A.D. 622 (A.H. 1). In the Moslem world, all dates are given in terms of the Hegira, which is generally abbreviated as A.H. in the same way that the Christian Era is indicated by the letters A.D. After the Hegira, the power of Mohammed rapidly increased, and in the eighth year after the Hegira, he began his march on Mecca at the head of ten thousand saints.

## The Night Journey

The celebrated Night Journey to Heaven is called the *Mi'raj*, which literally means an *ascent*. It is said to have occurred in the twelfth year of the Prophet's mission, about a year before the establishment of the Moslem era. Although the Koran contains no account of this event, it is supported

Mohammed's Night Journey to Heaven. 15th Century example in the early writing of a Tartaric tribe. This remarkable manuscript in the Bibliotheque Royale at Paris, includes the lives of the seventy-two Imams, or miracle-working saints. In the illustration, Mohammed is riding upon Al Borak, and accompanied by the Angel Gabriel. From *Universal Palaeography* by M. J. B. Silvestre.

by the seventeenth Sura, which may be freely translated: "Praise to Him who carried His servant by night from the temple of Mecca to the temple of Jerusalem." \*

On the occasion of the vision, Ayesha, who was then married to the Prophet, is quoted as authority that Mohammed's physical body did not disappear, but that God carried him away by night in the spirit. Most pious Moslems have held the validity of the vision, at least as a mystical experience, and as such, it cannot be assailed without directly attacking the integrity of Mohammed. This would appear unreasonable in view of his lifelong reputation for absolute honesty and sincerity. Washington Irving sets forth the essential features of the Night Journey, although he admits that he has not presented the story in its full amplitude.

On a certain night, described as the darkest and the most silent that the world had ever known, Mohammed was roused from his sleep by the angel Gabriel, who brought to the Prophet a strange and wonderful creature different from any which existed in the natural world. This creature had a human face, the body of a horse, the wings of an eagle, and eyes as radiant as the stars. It was female, and because of its dazzling splendor and incredible speed, it was called *Al Borak,* or *The Lightning.* Mounted on Al Borak, the Prophet was carried over Mount Sinai, upon which God spoke to Moses, and also Bethlehem, where Jesus, the son of Mary, was born. Accompanied by Gabriel, they arrived finally at the Holy Temple of Jerusalem. After dismounting from his flying steed, Mohammed entered the temple, and found there Abraham, Moses, Jesus, and many more of the prophets. According to a work by E. Dinet and Sliman ben Ibrahim,† Mohammed was met, on his arrival at Jerusalem, by a man holding forth a cup of wine and a cup of milk. Mohammed chose milk and Gabriel approved, saying that had he chosen wine, his people would have preferred error to truth.

---

\* See *Sufism,* by A. J. Arberry.
† See *The Life of Mohammed.*

Mohammed joined in prayer with Jesus and the ancient prophets for a considerable time. At the end of their sacred exercises, the sky seemed to open and a ladder of light was let down from heaven until the lower end of it rested on the stone, which is called the Rock Moriah. Assisted by the angel Gabriel, Mohammed ascended the ladder with strange ease and rapidity. In this vision, the celestial regions were divided into seven zones, which correspond with the orbits of the seven planets in the system of astronomy developed by Claudius Ptolemy of Alexandria. When the prophet arrived at the first heaven, Gabriel knocked at the gate. A voice from within then demanded, "Who is there?" And the angel replied that it was Gabriel, and that with him was Mohammed. The Guardian of the Gate then asked if the Prophet had already received his mission, and when this was answered in the affirmative, he was made welcome and the gate was opened to receive him. The first heaven was of silver, and the stars were suspended from the vault by chains of gold. In each star an angel was placed who acted as sentinel. As Mohammed entered, his forefather Adam appeared as an aged man. The Prophet paid homage to the first mortal, and Adam embraced his descendant. This region was also filled with many kinds of animals. Gabriel explained that these animals were really angels who, having taken on the forms of countless creatures, interceded with God for all the species of animals upon earth.

Gabriel and Mohammed then ascended to the second heaven, where they were received by Noah, the Patriarch of the Deluge, who embraced the Prophet with the greatest of kindness. In each case, the ritual of knocking at the gate and of being questioned was repeated. In the third heaven, was seated an Angel of immeasurable height, and Gabriel explained that this was Asrael, the Angel of Death. In the fourth heaven, they found the Angel of Tears, who wept over the sins of the children of men. The fifth heaven was of the finest gold, and here Mohammed was met and embraced by Aaron, and here also dwelt the Avenging Angel,

# THE MYSTICS OF ISLAM

Mosque of Omar in Jerusalem. It stands on the site of Herod's Temple.

who presided over the element of fire. The sixth heaven was composed of an immense transparent stone resembling a carbuncle. Here was a great Angel who was guardian of heaven and earth, and here also was stationed the Prophet Moses. Ascending still higher, Mohammed came to the seventh heaven, where he was received by the Patriarch Abraham. This wonderful place was formed of the Divine Light, and was of such transcendent glory that the tongue of man cannot describe it. Here there was a sacred house resembling the Kaaba at Mecca, which was suspended directly above the physical building. The order of the Patriarchs in this vision is changed in different accounts, and this will be considered in the analysis of the meaning of the Night Journey.

From the seventh heaven, the Prophet continued his strange journey, passing through a region of light and another of utter darkness. From this gloom he emerged to find himself in the presence of God, but the face of Allah was covered with twenty thousand veils. From the veils Deity put forth his hands, placing one upon the breast, and the other upon the shoulder of Mohammed. On this occasion many doctrines and prayers were communicated to the Prophet. The nature of the instruction is not recorded, but is said to have been preserved as part of the secret tradition in Islam. Mohammed then descended again by the golden ladder to the temple at Jerusalem, where he found Al Borak fastened as he had left her, and was then carried back to the place whence he had come.*

It will be noted that in his summary of the Night Journey, Washington Irving, for some reason, fails to name the Prophets who received Mohammed at certain of the gates. Several lists are available. According to one, for example, Mohammed met the ancient wise men in the following order: Adam, Noah, Aaron, Moses, Abraham, David, Solomon, Idris (Enoch), Yahya (John the Baptist), and Jesus. In this arrangement, it is implied that the total number of Prophets exceeded the number of the heavens; therefore, two or more must have occupied one sphere. Among other alternative lists found in the early commentaries, the seven gates of the seven heavens were attended by the holy ones in the following order: Adam, John and Jesus, Joseph, Enoch, Aaron, Moses, and Abraham. In the significant arrangement, which places Jesus at the gate of the seventh heaven, each of the older patriarchs asks Mohammed to intercede for him before the throne of God; but, reaching the sphere of Jesus, the situation is reversed, and Mohammed asks the Nazarene to intercede for him.

According to Godfrey Higgins, whose learning in comparative religion was prodigious, Mohammed, by asking Jesus to intercede for him at the seventh gate, placed Jesus Christ

---

* Digested from Washington Irving's *Mahomet and His Successors*, unless otherwise noted.

above himself, and indirectly but clearly declared himself a Christian. Higgins writes: "This is in perfect accordance with the Mohammedan doctrine — that through the excessive depravity of man, the mission of Jesus — of love — of peace — of benevolence — having failed, a strong one — that of the sword — must follow." * Due to the extraordinary nature of the vision, it was only reasonable that the details should be altered by various sects in different times, so as to conform with prevailing attitudes or serve for the introduction of esoteric and symbolical contemplation.

The Sufi Bengalee, in summarizing the importance of the Night Journey to the pious Moslem, states: "This vision was of enormous spiritual significance. The Ascension to Heaven meant that the Prophet's cause was destined to triumph. Secondly, that he would make the highest spiritual progress and would leave all behind in his nearness to God. The seven heavens meant that the path of spiritual journey was to be traversed gradually, and *step by step*." † This Sufi, in harmony with the natural inclinations of this highly metaphysical sect, also affirms that the ascension to heaven was definitely a mystical experience, or, as he calls it, a mental vision, and he quotes several Moslem authorities to support this conviction.

From Irving's account, together with certain additional material, it can be strongly suspected that the Night Journey involves the ritualism of an esoteric or mystical society. The description of the ornamentations of the seven spheres or levels suggests the decorations of a Lodge or sanctuary of initiatory rites. For example, in the first heaven, the stars are suspended from the sky by golden chains. This would scarcely be so specifically noted in a simple vision of the universal mystery, but would be necessary in a physical sanctuary where ritualism was performed. The Night Journey itself is highly reminiscent of the Apocalyptical vision

---

\* *Anacalypsis.*
† *The Life of Muhammad.*

of St. John, the account of the ascent through the seven spheres described by Hermes in the *Divine Pymander,* and the descent of Ishtar through the seven gates in the Babylonian legend of Tammuz. There is also a similar description of the wonders accompanying the delivery of the tablets of the Law to Moses on the flaming peak of Sinai. A cloud appeared which, opening like a mouth or door, permitted Moses to walk out upon the firmament, where he beheld the angels, came into the presence of God, was permitted to behold the seven heavens and the celestial tabernacle which was later to hover in the sky above the Everlasting House of Solomon the King.

It can only be assumed that a common tradition underlies all these accounts, and this tradition provides the basic structure upon which the initiatory pageantries and dramas were constructed. Certainly, the mysteries of Mithras, with their journey through the seven worlds, the rites of Samothrace, and the mortuary rituals of the Egyptians, which included the interrogation of the soul by the guardians of the gates of the underworld, fall in this archetypal concept. As Anubis conducted the souls of Egypt's dead, and Virgil led Dante through the inferno, there is always a companion or a guide to speak for the candidate until he has received the secret words of the degrees. In the case of Mohammed, Gabriel occupies this place. The Night Journey, therefore, is a valid landmark of the Adept Tradition, revealing beyond question that those fashioning the account, whether it was Mohammed himself or his early disciples, were following an established concept and bestowing it as a key to their teachings upon those of the faithful who came after them.

## *The Rise of Islam*

The eighth year after his flight into Medina, Mohammed reentered Mecca after what was intended to be a bloodless victory over his foes. Because certain of his followers disobeyed him, there were thirteen casualties. The march on Mecca began on the tenth day of the month of Ramadan, and when the Prophet entered the city, he carried a standard made of the black veil of his wife. Having circled the ancient Kaaba seven times, he ordered the images worshiped there, probably the *Lat* and *Uzza,* to be cast down. Mohammed then rededicated the temple, establishing the precedent for the annual pilgrimage to the Holy City.

Two years later, in the tenth year of the Hegira, Mohammed led what has been called the Valedictory Pilgrimage. For the last time, he rode at the head of the faithful upon his great black camel. The premonition of death was strong upon him, and it was his most devout desire that this pilgrimage should be the perfect model for the thousands that would follow in the course of centuries. During this last visit to the sacred city of his faith, the Prophet is said to have spoken frequently from the pulpit in the Kaaba, and in the open air from the back of his great camel. There is a legend, unsubstantiated, but certainly held in regard by the faithful, that during one of his sermons, the heavens opened and the voice of God was heard saying, "This day I have perfected your religion, and accomplished in you my grace." When these words were uttered, the assembled throng knelt in admiration and Mohammed's camel fell upon its knees and lowered its head to the earth.

The Prophet suffered much physical pain in the closing years of his life as the result of an effort made to poison him at Kheibar in the seventh year after the Hegira. Although he was miraculously prevented from eating the food, he had tasted of it, and the poison continued the slow work for which it was intended. Mohammed passed at Medina in the eleventh year of the Hegira (632 A.D.). His last words were remembered by Ayesha, his young wife of twenty years. Shortly before his passing, the Prophet prayed in a whisper: "Lord grant me pardon; and join me to the companionship on high!" Then, at brief intervals, he murmured, "Eternity in Paradise!" "Pardon!" "Yes; the blessed companionship on high!" Then, with a soft sigh, he expired.

Mohammed was buried beneath the floor of the room in which he died. This chamber is now called the Hujrah, and was originally the private apartment of Ayesha. The present state of the grave is described thus: "Above the Hujrah is the green dome, surmounted by a large gilt crescent, springing from a series of globes. Within the building are the tombs of Muhammad, Abu Bakr, and 'Umar, with a space reserved for the grave of our Lord Jesus Christ, whom Muslims say will again visit the earth, and die and be buried at al-Madinah. The grave of Fatima, the Prophet's daughter, is supposed to be in a separate part of the building, although some say she was buried at Baqi'. The Prophet's body is said to be stretched full length on the right side, with the right palm supporting the right cheek, the face fronting Mekkah. Close behind him is placed Abu Bakr, whose face fronts Muhammad's shoulder, and then 'Umar, who occupies the same position with respect to his predecessor. Amongst Christian historians, there was a popular story to the effect that Muhammadans believed the coffin of their Prophet to be suspended in the air, which has no foundation whatever in Muslim literature, and Niebuhr thinks that the story must have arisen from the rude pictures sold to strangers." \*

After the passing of the Prophet, the succession of Islam was vested in the Caliphate. The nature of this institution has been subject to many conflicting accounts, and some Moslem sects hold it in slight esteem. Generally, however, it is regarded as according to the will of the Prophet. In the Sunni writings, which represent the words of the Companions of the House of the Prophet, a Caliph must be a man who has attained adulthood, a sane person, a free man, a learned divine, a powerful ruler, a just governor, and belonging to the tribe from which the Prophet himself descended. Some hold that a Caliph must be descended from the family

---

\* *A Dictionary of Islam.*

of the Prophet. Several elements contribute to the suitability of a candidate making claim for the Caliphate. First of all, he must be the *de facto* holder of the title for which no better claimant has appeared. He must be in a political or military position to support his claim. He must be elected through the sanction of a legal body of elders. Second, he must, if possible, receive the right of succession from a previous holder whose position was unquestioned. Third, he should be the guardian of the two shrines, Mecca and Jerusalem, and he must have the possession of the sacred relics: the cloak of the Prophet, the hairs from the Prophet's beard, and the sword of the Caliph 'Umar.\*

As the whole subject of the Caliphate is exceedingly complicated, it may be as well to summarize it by a direct quotation from a Moslem writer. "The succession of Muslim sovereigns varied. Abu Bakr, the first successor of the Prophet, was chosen by the most influential party in the Muslim community: Omar ('Umar) was designated by Abu Bakr; Othman, by electors whom Omar had named; the election of Ali led to civil war; with Muawiya the dynastic rule was established, first in the family of the Umayyads. Even in the dynasties, the order of succession was not always constant. Sometimes the Caliph chose one of his sons as his heir-apparent; for example, Haroum-ur Rashid designated three of his sons with entail. The first of the three, Al-Amin, wished to oust the second, Al-Mamun; but the latter revolted and Al-Amin was killed. Among the Ottoman Sultans it was rather the brother who succeeded." †

The functions of a Caliph are also vaguely defined. Theoretically, this dignitary is the vice-regent or deputy of the Prophet. In the Koran, the word *Caliph* is used in reference to Adam, who was regarded as the vice-regent of the Most High. David is also mentioned as a Caliph. In practical terms, however, the Caliph can function only within certain

---

\* For further details, see *The Future of Islam* by Wilfred Scawen Blunt.
† *Islam in the World*, by Zaki Ali.

arbitrary boundaries unless he is strong enough and exercises sufficient personal glamor to attain autocracy by the consent of the governed. In principle, all legislation is based upon the will of God. The laws of Deity are revealed through the Koran. Next in authority are the traditions derived from the words of the Companions of the Prophet and certain immediate commentaries thereon. This body of instruction is known as the *Sunni*. Finally, authority is vested in the consensus. The Caliph can be duly invested only with legislative prerogatives by the express will of the entire Moslem community or nation. Finally, therefore, the proofs of the Caliphate are, at least theoretically, nomination by the preceding Caliph and the voluntary acceptance by a pronouncement of the people.

From the early Caliphs, and some outstanding leaders of later times, the principal sects of the Moslems derived their names and authorities. One by one, the various dynasties had their days. Some enjoyed comparatively slight power and influence; others endured for a long time. Around each, legends have sprung up, and these, weaving together through the centuries, form the elaborate pattern of Moslem philosophy, theology, and history. Also at this time, the term *Imam* must be introduced. By most conservative interpretations, the word *Imam* is regarded as synonymous with *Caliph*. The moment such a leader transgresses the laws of the Koran, or fails in the traditional virtues and benevolences of his office, it is the duty of the faithful to reject him or replace him, and to deny that he is their true leader.

According to the Sunni, those who cling to the tradition acknowledging the first four Caliphs, the Caliph is the true Imam. But the more mystical sect of the Shi'ahs applies the term *Imam* to the seven or twelve leaders of their own sect, and among them an elaborate metaphysical doctrine has developed. The Imams of this sect descend from Ali, the son-in-law of the Prophet, through the eldest son of Ali and Fatima. Their second son, Al-Husain was the third Imam, and his son was the fourth. The twelfth and last Imam, who is yet to come, will be named Mohammed. It is believed that he has been alive for centuries, but lives in secrecy. When the proper day comes, he will appear among the faithful as the Mahdi, the comforter of the last day, whose advent was predicted by the Prophet.

Bernard H. Springett gives a ray of insight into the Imam concept. "The Persian kings of the Sufee dynasty styled themselves 'slaves of the Lord of the Country,' that is, of the invisible Imaums; they always kept two horses saddled and bridled in the royal sables at Isfahan, one for the twelfth Imaum, whenever he should appear, the other for Jesus Christ, by whom they believed he would be accompanied." *

*Religious Philosophy in Islam*

This is not a general study of Moslemism, but a section of an encyclopedic survey dealing with the descent of the Adept Tradition among the various religions of the world. It cannot be said that all of the members of these faiths are in common agreement upon the esoteric aspects of their own beliefs. Many Christians reject Christian mysticism, although it has been taught and accepted by the most illustrious and venerated leaders of the faith. Many orthodox Jews have been taught to regard the Cabala as dangerous and unlawful, yet it cannot be denied that speculations based upon its elaborate symbolism have dominated the interests of many Rabbis and scholars. It would not be appropriate for a non-Moslem, therefore, to speak for the faith of these people, or to dogmatize upon its doctrines. It is intended in this work to point out the parallels between certain aspects of Near Eastern metaphysics and the universal belief in the existence of sanctified persons possessing extraordinary insight into the mysteries of God.

---

* *Secret sects of Syria and the Lebanon.*

It is extremely difficult to draw a comprehensive picture of the more subtle aspects of Moslem religion and philosophy from the attitudes and opinions of non-Moslem authors. The general attitude of the European writers toward the faith of Islam has been, for the most part, extremely critical. No other living religion has been so openly and aggressively attacked. As this policy has long endured, and is present on many levels of thought, it must be suspected that most available accounts are to some degree prejudiced, even though the writers themselves declare their impartiality or even sympathy.

The impact of Islam on the Christian world was unfortunately timed. It occurred during the Dark Ages, when Europe was under the heavy clouds of intolerance and illiteracy. The Christian world stood aghast at the audacity of Mohammed, when he claimed that he had been commissioned by God to succeed the earlier teachers, and further unfold the mysteries of the true faith. Here, then, was a vast and growing heresy which even the Crusades could not stamp out, and which for centuries threatened to overwhelm Europe. Devout medieval theologians prayed to heaven for deliverance from the plague, the Turk, and the comet.

Today the faith of Islam is firmly established in most parts of the world. After analyzing the distribution of Moslems according to continents and nations, Zaki Ali concludes: ". . . it may be safely assumed that there about 400 million Muslims in the world." * Under conditions as they now exist, there is every inducement for understanding and appreciation between the principal faiths of mankind, and it is on the level of mysticism, with its deep and generous understanding of values, that this union can most naturally and easily be accomplished.

There is no doubt that Mohammed had learned of the

---

* *Islam in the World.*

lamentable procedures which in his day were disfiguring the rise of the Christian church. There gradually integrated within his own consciousness the concept of a natural religion, a faith of extreme simplicity in which there was slight possibility of elaborate controversies or feuds or schismatic quarrels. He did not believe that men should be divided by the transcendental elements of creeds. About that which cannot be seen or known with certainty, little satisfaction can be gained by argument. The Prophet was an Arab among Arabs. He knew their ways, and he recognized their needs. To him, it was far better that the conduct of the individual should be wisely and lovingly directed along familiar paths rather than that he be involved in disputes which might well cause him to live destructively and intemperately in the name of religion.

The outcome of the Prophet's personal spiritual experience was a faith for the men of the desert. These were the men who kept the sheep and journeyed along the caravan routes. They should be honorable in their dealings, charitable in their inclinations, and they should be able to pray side by side, seeking the strength of heaven in time of sorrow or danger. What simpler theology could be devised than the basic substance of Islam? There is no God but God; worship him with a full heart. There is one law; keep it with contrition of spirit. There is one humanity; cooperate in all things for the common good. Mohammed sincerely believed that if these essentials were honestly cultivated, there would be no more theological despotism. Unfortunately, he was not able to so completely instill his teachings into the hearts of his own people that they could live the fullness of his message. This should not be regarded as his fault, however, but rather the common weakness of all flesh.

The early relationships between the rising Moslem world and the followers of the Jewish and Christian faiths were not essentially difficult or unhappy. Mohammed designated the Jews and Christians as the people of the Book, referring to the Bible. In his time, of course, the Koran had not been integrated. The Moslem was therefore dependent upon the words of a living teacher for his spiritual instruction. Gradually, a contrast was established and the Moslems considered themselves the people of the family, or the household, with Mohammed as their common father. The Prophet forbade the persecution of any man for his faith, so long as he lived it with sincerity of spirit, but he did regard it as virtuous and necessary that the Moslem should defend his own belief against oppression and tyranny. If he were attacked, he should use every possible means to achieve victory and to discomfit his adversary. If, however, his adversary surrendered, or asked for peace, there should be no spirit of vengeance. Again, unfortunately, human nature was stronger than revelation.

For most of the differences which seem inevitably to arise in the evolution of religions, Mohammed had a simple remedy. "If God had pleased, he had surely made you one people; but he has thought fit to try you in that which he has given you. Therefore, strive to excel each other in good works: unto God shall ye all return, and then he will declare unto you that concerning which ye have disagreed."*

The conflict between early Moslem and Christian teachings may be said to have strengthened both faiths, but it also increased the barriers between them. In the world of Islam, however, there was little indication of a broad tendency toward religious persecution. The early Moslem was permitted to marry Christians and to share food with them, and these acts were regarded as certain evidence of basic tolerance. Both Christians and Jews were elevated to high office, and were respected for their attainments in medicine, art, literature, law, and science. Under the Caliphs there was a brilliant restoration of learning, centering in Baghdad, Cairo, and other important Moslem cities. Other elements also began to emerge from the original focus of Islamic ideology. Conflict impelled the Moslem to strengthen his own

---

* Koran, Sura V: 53.

doctrinal position, seek to define orthodoxy, and prevent, so far as was possible, the breaking away of schismatic sects.

Obviously, the Koran, though a work of great spiritual insight and gracious literary style, could not meet all the requirements of the proud civilization that was rising in Asia Minor and North Africa. The scholar and the natural mystic also had requirements peculiar to their natures, and it was inevitable that Islam, like all other religions, should divide into an esoteric and exoteric part, the former drifting toward metaphysical speculation, and the latter retaining a conservative and orthodox allegiance to the letter of the revealed law.

Because Islamism is a strict monotheistic faith, it emphasizes the need for saints or intermediaries between God and man. This is the same situation that led to the Buddhist veneration for Arhats or illumined teachers. Godfrey Higgins refers to a secret doctrine taught by Pythagoras, Jesus, and Mohammed. Always and everywhere, such a doctrine is associated with the concepts of a hierarchy of initiate-teachers, advanced beyond the state of ordinary mortals. These are not divine beings in any sense of the word, or Islam would not and could not have accepted them. Rather, they are sanctified mortals, who have attained a divine insight through faithful observance of the esoteric disciplines of their orders, and who have become vigilant guardians over the spiritual destinies of uninitiated mortals.

In reply to the question as to whether the followers of Mohammed actually accepted an Adept Hierarchy, John P. Brown, an outstanding authority on Moslem secret societies, writes: "The Dervish Order put full faith in all the grades of spiritually superior men and angelic beings. The former composed what are ordinarily termed saints, or friends of Allah. These, in the Koran are designated as 'the friends of God who fear nothing; they are not subject to any affliction, because they entertain the true faith; they have lived consistently with it, and in exact obedience with God, from whom they receive a reward in this life and in the other.' 'They are the title of the book of the law of God; the demonstration of all the truths and mysteries of faith; their external appearance leads us to an observance of the laws of God, and their interior incites us to abandon and detach ourselves from all the pleasures of this world.' 'They commenced their career before the beginning of time, and labor only for eternity.' 'During their lives they never left the portals of the sacred palace of the Divinity, and finally enter therein.' 'They discover and behold the spiritual secrets which God reveals to them, and maintain therein a religious silence.' "*

According to certain mystical calculations, the true saints of the Moslem world are called The Three, The Five, The Seven, and The Forty. These are the "unseen men" who journey to all parts of the world according to the Will of God and are given authority over the affairs of mankind, both Moslem and non-Moslem. Sometimes these saints are collectively referred to as The Owners, or Masters of Destiny. The chief among them is known as the Center, and each morning, the saints assemble at Mecca, presumably by some mystical projection of their higher natures, and report all they have learned and done to the Center. On these occasions, there is a religious rite of prayer and dedication, and they then return to their proper labors. The various mystical orders are the gates of the eternal city of Wisdom which, according to the sayings attributed to the Prophet, is that vast community of the sages where the blessed dwell in their conditions of attainment.

Nearly always, extraordinary achievements in arts and sciences bear witness to the rise of metaphysical speculation. This is especially true when the life of a people is bound intimately to its revealed religion, which is the dynamics behind all progress and achievement. *The Library of Original Sources* thus summarizes the early accomplishments of

---

\* *The Dervishes.*

the Moslems: "The results of Mohammedism have been greatly underestimated. In the century after Mohammed's death, it wrested Asia Minor, Africa and Spain from Christianity, more than half of the civilized world, and established a civilization, the highest in the world during the dark ages. It brought the Arabian race to their highest development, raised the position of woman in the East, though it retained polygamy, was intensely monotheistic, and until the Turks gained control, for the most part encouraged progress." *

In his work, *Islam in the World,* Dr. Zaki Ali summarizes the scientific, ethical, and educational achievements of Islamic civilization, with special reference to the state of Spain under Moslem rule. He points out that in the 10th century, the population of the city of Cordova was computed at about one million. At this time, under the Moors, Cordova had fifty hospitals, nine hundred public baths, eight hundred schools, six hundred mosques, and a library of six hundred thousand volumes, in addition to seventy private libraries. The same author gives a description of the establishment of infirmaries for the blind and for lepers at Damascus. The great ruler, Haroum-al Rashid established a tradition of his own by attaching a college and hospital to every mosque. He opened an asylum for the insane, and it is universally admitted that those mentally ill were treated with much more humanity and far greater wisdom in Islamic hospitals than in European hospitals of a much later date. In the 10th century, many hospitals appeared in the city of Baghdad, each under the direction of a renowned and skillful physician. Inspectors were appointed to make certain that there was no abuse or mismanagement in these institutions. In the 12th century, a Jewish traveler, Benjamin of Tudela, passing through Baghdad, found sixty hospitals, all adequately supported from the king's stores. Every patient asking for assistance was given the best of food and care until the cure was completed.

---

* Vol. IV, Section: "The Era of the Arabs."

Speaking of Haroum-Al Rashid, W. Wilson Cash writes: "Owing to the conquest of Jerusalem by the Arabs, Haroum Al-Rashid had in possession the keys of the Church of the Holy Sepulchre at Jerusalem. These he dispatched to Charlemagne, the representative of Christianity in the West, an act that was meant to seal a new friendship between East and West, Islam and Christianity." * There can be no doubt that the early leaders of Islam sought to advance the securities of their own people and to bridge the religious interval between their faith and the religions of surrounding peoples. Everything depended upon the genius of inspired leadership. Under good men, virtue triumphed, but with the passing of time, power and luxury undermined the simple austerity of Mohammed's personal example. This changing of times, combined with the increasing resentment of Western peoples, brought about a tragedy of misunderstanding which was climaxed in one of the most disgraceful episodes in recorded history — the cycle of the Crusades.

From the time of the conquests of Genghis Khan (1162-1227), splendid empires flourished beyond the Euphrates. Over these incredible conglomerates ruled magnificent tyrants, some benevolent and others cruel and ignorant. Many were richly endowed with abilities and capacities, and nearly all of them were better educated and more thoughtful than their Western contemporaries. While the kings of Europe still made their marks on official documents or had their own edicts written for them and read back to them by hired scribes, the princes of Asia were endowing libraries, studying the stars, publishing editions of Plato and Euclid, and encouraging art and literature. Most of these Eastern empire-builders were devout Moslems, and while they did not allow their belief to interfere with their territorial ambitions, they had the wisdom and the wit to govern their peoples by means of surprisingly lofty ethical codes.

---

* *The Moslem World in Revolution.*

## Timur Shah

The mingling of mystical religious ideas with powerful political programs is clearly revealed in the case of Timur Shah (Timur I Leng). This ruler, better known as Tamerlane, the Shaker of the Earth, was born in 1336 (?) at Kesh in Transoiana, a region now included in the U.S.S.R. Republic of Uzbek. Through his mother, he was the great-grandson of Genghis Khan, and, like his illustrious ancestor, was originally a petty tribal chieftain in the neighborhood of Samarkand. His career developed around the concept that there was only one God in heaven, so there should be only one ruler on earth, and in 1369, at Samarkand, he was proclaimed sovereign over a conglomeration of peoples. Convinced that he was to be a master of the world, he followed the traditional policy of conquest, and most of his life was devoted to military campaigning. Like many Asiatic princes, however, he combined the attributes of a despot with those of a scholar. Ruthless in warfare, he was devoted to art, music, and literature, and having become master of a region, governed it with tolerance and wisdom.

It is known that Timur was a profound student of the Koran as early as his twentieth year. He was acquainted with the numerous commentaries upon the basic writings of Islam which had been prepared by mystical sects, and he was much given to metaphysical speculations. According to Eastern records, Timur left several manuscripts, of which the most important are the *Memoires* and *Institutes*. Timur died at Ortar in 1405. His body was embalmed with rose water and musk, enclosed within an ebony casket, and returned to Samarkand for burial. By the time of his death, his empire extended from the Great Wall of China to the frontier of Asia Minor, and from the Sea of Aral to the Ganges and the Persian Gulf. He was contemplating a campaign against China at the time of his demise. In the

Illumination representing Timur Shah receiving the homage of a conquered king. Probably 19th Century.

creation of his vast domain, according to one writer,* he extinguished twenty-seven separate states and nine dynasties.

The books written by Timur were discovered after a diligent search, and presented to the Mogul emperor, Shah Jahan, in 1637. Critical Western scholars are inclined to some doubts and reservations about the authenticity of the writings attributed to Timur, but they have been generally accepted by Eastern historians. A translation of the *Institutes*, etc., of Timur was made by Joseph White, D.D., and published at Oxford in 1783. The English version is unusually sympathetic, considering its source, and we must recognize Dr. White as an honorable and careful scholar. Unfortunately, this translation is scarce, and it has not received the consideratioin and approbation which the text deserves.

From the *Institutes* it would appear that Timur leaned heavily for advice and judgment upon a mysterious sage whom he called his "ghostly father." In the text, this elusive sage is consistently referred to as "The Peer," a word of Arabic extraction which signifies all that is venerable. In moments of emergency, and especially on such occasions as required broad policies for the just administration of conquered territories, this Peer communicated with Timur, and several of his letters reveal lofty and noble sentiments. Summarizing the contributions of this remarkable and sanctified scholar, Dr. White writes: "Koottub ul Aktuab Sheikh Zine u deen Aboo Bukkur a devout and learned man descended from the Mahummudan Lawgiver, who foretold to Timur the power and greatness to which he would arise. It appears that this prince considered him in the light of a ghostly father, consulted him on all occasions, and paid the most implicit attention to his counsels." It would seem that this wonderful philosopher was a Dervish, a member of a sect for which Timur had special regard. *The Book of the Adepts,* so highly prized by the Dervishes, has numerous

---

* See *Studies in Indian Painting* by Nanalal C. Mehta.

references to these shadowy saints who guided the rise of the Moslem spiritual and temporal powers.

Timur surrounded himself with scientists and prominent intellectuals. In one place he writes: "And, with the assistance of astrology, I ascertained the benign or malignant aspect of the stars; their motions, and the revolutions of the heavens."

When Timur developed a system of government based almost entirely upon existing knowledge of astronomy and astrology, he established a precedent of considerable political interest. He divided the peoples within his domains into twelve groups, according to their trades, professions, and social conditions. He then set to work to unfold through these groups the potentials symbolized by the constellations. Later Timur placed over each of the divisions a counselor or leader, who was responsible to him for the people whom each directed. There was also a privy council, analogous to the planets, and this operated through all classes. Finally, this remarkable person imposed upon himself twelve rules, based also upon astrological concepts, convinced that only by governing his own conduct was he entitled to rule over others.

Timur learned discretion and discrimination through a hazardous career. His practical teachers were trial and error. He might not have done so well had he not received counsel from his "ghostly father." This wise old Dervish reminded Timur that it is one thing to build an empire, and quite another thing to preserve it. Courage builds, but only discretion preserves. Stronger even than the powerful person of the prince is the code of laws, which must survive him and continue to serve the people after he has gone. Weak men elevated to high positions can sometimes preserve the state if the laws are strong and just.

## Akbar the Great

Reference should certainly be made to Akbar the Great, Emperor of Hindustan (1542-1605). In the nature of this extraordinary man, personal ambitions and impersonal aspirations were strangely and intimately mingled. Of him, C. W. King writes: "Again, the greatest of all Mohammedan sovereigns, the Mogul Akbar, was a true *Sufi;* equally so was his prime minister and historian, Abul Farez. It would be difficult to find in a modern Christian prayerbook, much less in any one composed in his age, an address to the Deity so sublime, so consonant with our present notions, as the invocation opening his *Ayeen-Akbari.* In all such outpourings of Oriental adoration, no allusion whatever to their special lawgiver is to be detected, nothing to betray any distinctive sectarian prejudice; the reader, if unacquainted with the history of the author, would admire, but know not what creed to adjudge the composition." *

To his brilliant court, Akbar invited representatives of many faiths, requiring of them mutual respect while in his presence. He was considerably influenced by Jesuit Fathers, and it was thought for a time that he intended to embrace Christianity. He was also thoughtful of the teachers of Hinduism, and was profoundly influenced by the faith of Zoroaster. Later, he investigated the claims of the Jains, and kept teachers of this sect at his court. His contact with the Sikhs was not so intimate, but he became proficient in their beliefs. Moved by a powerful desire to unite the spiritual convictions of mankind and bring to an end the discords and antagonisms of faiths, he founded, at Fatehpur-Sikri, his House of Worship. After describing the construction of this building, Sir Laurence Binyon reports thus upon the meetings held there: "So it was ordained that on the south side should sit the Learned Doctors; on the north, the

---

* *The Gnostics and Their Remains.*

Ascetics and Mystics; on the west, reputed descendants of the Prophet; on the east, such Nobles as cared for these matters. And Akbar presided over them all; not enthroned in immovable dignity, but moving in his restless way freely among them, and talking now with one and now with another."*

Although Akbar's religious experiment was essentially unsuccessful, it indicates the natural workings of his mind, and his desire to fulfill a deep spiritual conviction. Sir Laurence Binyon mentions mystical experiences which occurred to Akbar, and it was also known that he came under the influence of learned mystics belonging to various Eastern and Near Eastern sects.

## The Foundations of Islamic Mysticism

Located at the crossroads of the ancient world, the Near East was a veritable alchemistical laboratory, in which elements of Asiatic and European doctrines mingled to form strange and unfamiliar compounds. Average members of religious organizations are seldom aware of the strange chemistry which creates faiths, crystallizes creeds, and formularizes dogmas. The story of religion is the account of numberless minglings of streams of human conviction, and all surviving creeds contain elements from numerous and widely scattered moral systems. In the Islamic complex of states and countries, the religion of Mohammed generated from within itself several important mystical sects. These sects, although dominated by the prevailing faith, found justification for existence by luminous explanations of obscure or controversial elements of the dominant faith. Sometimes these dependent sects inclined to be more materialistic than the parent religion, but more often, they

---

* *Akbar.*

unfolded and enriched spiritual overtones, and inclined to asceticism or strict observance.

The Moslem is a devout person who keeps the letter of his creed more consistently than the followers of most other religious groups. But even the merchant is a poet in his heart, and shares the Asiatic inclination to dramatize his spiritual convictions. Many strange forms of learning flourished in the Near East, and emancipated Christian intellectuals were perfectly willing to hazard their reputations, and even to endanger their lives, by studying with Islamic masters and dabbling in the magical arts of the Arabs, Moors, and Saracens.

Among the most interesting of the mystical groups of southwestern Asia are the Druses of Syria and the Lebanon, and the Dervishes and the Sufis, who originated in the Persian-Arabian region and have extended their influence throughout the Moslem world. The origin and ethnological affinity of the Druses is as yet unknown. Although they speak Arabic with admirable correctness, the main body of this group does not belong to the Semitic family. They like to regard themselves as unitarians, and many of them are described as "fair-haired, of light complexion, strong and well-made, and often as tall as northern Europeans." * At the present time, they follow in general the custom and culture of their Moslem neighbors.

Most writers have not clearly distinguished between the Dervishes and the Sufis. John P. Brown, an authority on these sects, treats the two groups without any clear differentiation. By way of definition, D. S. Margoliouth writes: "In general, we may distinguish between *Sufi* and Dervish as between theory and practice; the former holds a certain philosophical doctrine, the latter practices a particular form of rite." † Stanley Lane-Poole, in his notes on the 10th

---

\* See *Encyclopedia Britannica* (1898)—"Druses."
† See *Encyclopedia of Religion and Ethics*—"Dervishes."

chapter of the Arabian Nights, states that there is an order of Moslem Dervishes called *Sufis*, who make a profession of more regular and more contemplative life than Dervishes in general, and many of this class have written books of spirituality, of devotion, and of contemplation.

Mystical sects in general are motivated by the desire for the personal experience of spiritual reality. With similar, if not identical objectives, the disciplines practiced to attain the enlargement and extension of consciousness are approximately the same, regardless of geographical distribution. Thus it is that the mystics are more inclined to be tolerant and to accept the fact of inter-religious unity. It is rare to find an advanced mystic who is not aware that all faiths have the same objective, and, broadly speaking, the same methods for the attainment of internal security.

Mystical religious movements founded by sincere and enlightened persons, and long sustained by devout and dedicated members, sometimes fall into evil days. The tendency of all religions is to drift away from their foundations, and to become involved in the materialistic ambitions of the masses. Few religions have endured for any great length of time without some measure of corruption. The faith depends upon the faithful for its vitality, and when the followers of a doctrine compromise its principles, and these compromises are in turn further compromised, the end is confusion. Mysticism represents a level of conviction difficult to maintain, and suitable only for those by nature sensitive and contemplative. So subtle are the values, that they are easily obscured, and the degree of this obscuration is difficult to estimate. Research is further complicated by the syncretic structure of mystical convictions. Usually the underlying concepts are derived from so many sources that it is almost impossible to determine what constitutes the essential elements of the pattern.

The study of Islamic metaphysics gradually leads to the conclusion that a marked change of world significance took place between the 10th and 13th centuries of the Christian era. Nearly all of the esoteric societies of the Moslem world developed within this period, and their leaders and founders appear to have been inspired by a common heritage of information. At this time, a group of schools arose in Islam involving elements of Platonism, Bactrian Buddhism, Syrian and Alexandrian Gnosticism, orthodox Judaism, unorthodox Cabalism, Moslem metaphysics, Aristotelian philosophy, Sabianism, and Iranian fire worship. The careful and astute ordering of these elements into a compound of religious, political, and philosophical significance, did not come about by accident, but by a thorough and careful plan. To appreciate this plan, the truth-seeker must penetrate a maze of records and reports, prejudiced and unprejudiced, reasonable and unreasonable, always bearing in mind that the Moslem was a sincere person, not inclined to corrupt his faith, but seeking rather to expand its sphere of influence and perfect its internal parts. For practical purposes, therefore, it seems appropriate at this time to explore the mystery of the House of Wisdom in Cairo.

## The House of Wisdom

One of the most extraordinary of all secret societies arose in Egypt in the 10th century A.D. The Caliph Abu Mohammed Abdallah claimed the caliphate because he was directly descended from Fatima, the daughter of the Prophet Mohammed. He broke away from the Abbasside Dynasty and founded the Fatimite Dynasty, establishing his throne at Cairo. The motives which impelled this bold action have never been adequately examined, but they must have been acceptable to a considerable number of devout Moslems or the new Dynasty could not have survived. In light of later events, it would appear that the Caliph Abdallah was a man of more than average intellectual attainments. The principal college in Cairo, the Dar-ul-Likmat (House of Science) was a distinguished center of learning, and to this the Caliph attached a Grand Lodge, dedicated to the advancement of philosophical and esoteric doctrines.* This was called the House of Wisdom, and here candidates for initiation into the mysteries of Ismaelism were regularly instructed. The instructions, which took the form of philosophical conferences, were given twice weekly, and both men and women attended this school. Wearing white robes, the neophytes and disciples were seated around the Grand Prior, who read to them discourses approved by the Caliph, who was the Grand Master of the Order.† Originally, Abdallah divided his system of initiation into seven degrees. The teachings of Pythagoras, Plato, and Aristotle, were included in the sacred curriculum, and aspirants advanced from one level of knowledge to another, only a few attaining to the ultimate teaching of the Lodge.

The principal historians of the House of Wisdom are Joseph von Hammer and Stanley Lane-Poole, both of whom showed marked prejudice against Moslem mysticism in general and the House of Wisdom in particular. It is generally admitted, however, that the seven basic degrees contributed to nobility of character, and the teachings included in them were above reproach.

The first degree was the longest and the most difficult, for it involved broad attainments in knowledge and most solemn obligations to the teacher and the Lodge. The second degree conveyed a knowledge of the Imams, whom Makrisi‡ describes as certain sacred beings or persons, the source of all knowledge, who appear at various times to preserve the holy doctrine. This gives the impression that the Imams were actually Adepts, the higher members of a spiritual over-government founded in the esoteric tradition of antiquity. The third degree gave the number of the holy Imams as

---

\* See *A Short History of the Saracens* by Amer Ali.
† *Secret Sects of Syria and the Lebanon* by Bernard H. Springett.
‡ Native authority quoted by von Hammer.

seven, and related this number to the seven heavens, the seven planets, the seven musical sounds, and all the other septenaries familiar to students of ancient symbolical philosophy. The fourth degree described the seven divine lawgivers, the apostles of God who had succeeded one another, beginning with Noah and Abraham. The fifth degree extended the secret knowledge to the consideration of the number twelve, taking up such matters as the twelve signs of the zodiac, the twelve tribes of Israel, and so forth. The sixth degree was essentially philosophical, with emphasis upon Plato, Aristotle, and Pythagoras. The seventh presented an Oriental mystical theology, including the doctrine of unity which the Sufis exhibited.

This program of instruction followed broadly the form of the philosophic ladder of Plotinus, the Alexandrian Neoplatonist. The disciple advances systematically through the abstract branches of learning, always dear to the Eastern heart, and while modern educators might consider the subject matter irregular, there would be no cause to question the piety of this Grand Lodge. To the original seven degrees, two additional phantom levels are said to have been added, and that the teaching of these completely destroyed the spirit and intent of the House of Wisdom. The Initiate was required to reject all the knowledge he had previously learned and cultivate total atheism. We are required to assume that the Moslems who attended the House of Wisdom would ultimately consent to beliefs and policies totally inconsistent with the doctrines of Mohammed. The average Moslem is a good man, and the scholars, philosophers, and mystics of Islam would never have sanctioned, even for a moment, a system of instruction which would open the teachings of their prophet to condemnation and ridicule. The most reasonable assumption is that the so-called eighth and ninth degrees were a fabrication intended to discredit a secret society with a wide sphere of influence. There is a parallel in Europe in the falsifications invented to justify the condemnation of the Knights Templars.

There is a reasonable possibility that the House of Wisdom may have practiced esoteric exercises, encouraged its members to detach themselves from wordly ambitions, and liberate their hearts and minds from the authority of tradition. The belief that material ambition is an illusion, worldly goods merely a burden upon the spirit, and extreme intellectualism a detriment to mystical insight, corresponded closely with the accepted teachings of the Dervishes and the Sufis. The House of Wisdom could have been influenced by Far Eastern sects which are known to have penetrated the area. In farther Asia, Buddhism and several schools of Hindu mysticism were persecuted by ambitious rulers because such ideals cannot be reconciled with tyranny.

Instead of assuming, as Lane-Poole did, that the House of Wisdom was attempting to destroy the religion of Islam, it may have been a valiant effort to restore the original mystical tradition in Islam. It is known that the simple moral code of the Prophet was being dangerously undermined by political conflicts over the Caliphate, or descent of leadership from the Prophet.

It was acknowledged that God was always represented in the material world by a spiritual leader called an *Imam*. It had become apparent, however, that the descent of the Imams had been historically broken, and it seemed that the spiritual security of the faithful was endangered. To meet this emergency, a doctrine was formulated by which the *Imam,* or spiritual leader, was not always visible, but was nevertheless present as a concealed, but all-powerful being. The hidden Imam, who was a secret ruler of the inner destiny of the Moslem world, would reveal himself to his faithful followers when the proper time arose. Meanwhile, it was the duty of those of good faith not only to await his coming, but to strive to hasten this event by personal piety.

The doctrine of the hidden Imam must be zealously preached, for in this mysterious being, all the secrets of the Most High were deposited and protected. It was proper that his missionaries should go forth, calling men to the truth, like Prophets in the wilderness.* As the concept of a coming world teacher is common to many religions, it cannot be held that this doctrine was essentially dangerous or heretical.

If this is the teaching which the House of Wisdom is accused of promulgating, it would seem that this secret society was actually a group of religious and philosophical reformers, who suffered the misfortune natural to such groups. To protect itself, the Society therefore subjected its disciples to initiations and tests, bound them to secrecy concerning the ultimate objectives, and encouraged them to spread the teachings throughout the Moslem world, including Arabia, Mesopotamia, and North Africa. These missionaries were called *da'is,* and they were carefully trained to teach in a manner understandable to the levels of society which they sought to influence. To the uneducated, they presented their ideas in simple form, based almost entirely upon the accepted morality of the Koran. To this they added only certain references to the coming of the Mahdi. For those more philosophically inclined, the groundwork of the concept was more carefully unfolded.

These missionaries were accused of appealing to members of various religions, and this is quite possible. If they firmly believed that they were the custodians of an esoteric plan for the union of faiths, the overthrow of tyranny, and the final liberation of the human mind from ignorance and fear, they would certainly not pause at the boundary lines of creeds. To assume that these teachers were all guilty of a gigantic hypocrisy is merely to reveal personal intolerance. There is much to indicate that the broad program of the House of Wisdom reached Europe, and influenced many progressive thinkers. It is believed to have assisted in the restoration of learning after the benightedness of the Dark Ages, becoming a center of arbitration for the disputes between Europe and Asia. It is suspected that the Florentine

---

* See *The Story of Cairo* by Stanley Lane-Poole.

Academy of Lorenzo de Medici was patterned after the Holy House of Cairo.

## The Arabian Nights Entertainment

The origin of a collection of ancient stories, legends, and traditions now called the *Arabian Nights Entertainment,* or *The Thousand and One Nights,* has been a subject of considerable speculation. All that can be said with certainty is that these stories were gathered from a variety of sources over a considerable period of time. Sir Richard Burton, whose name has long been associated with the English translation of these Oriental tales, concluded that the author or authors responsible for the writings are unknown. Burton, therefore, is in substantial agreement with other editors and translators who have explored the same field. It appears most "unlikely" that the work was subject to any early editorial policy. There are many diversified themes and clearly distinguishable levels of literary ability. Certain diverse chronological references in the text have also inclined learned interpreters and tranlators to take refuge in the opinion that the stories simply accumulated without rhyme or reason.

In the "Terminal Essay" appended to his translation of *The Thousand and One Nights,* Burton attempts to analyze, out of his broad knowledge of Arabian culture, the background and historical descent of this famous collection of Near-Eastern stories. Summarizing the nature of the people among whom these tales originated, he says: "Considered in a higher phase, the medieval Moslem mind displays, like the ancient Egyptian, a most exalted moral idea, the deepest reverence for all things connected with his religion and a sublime conception of the Unity and Omnipotence of the Deity." On the negative side of the picture, Burton is no less exact: "Our Arab at his worst is a mere barbarian who has not forgotten the savage. He is a model mixture of childishness and astuteness, of simplicity and cunning, concealing levity of mind under solemnity of aspect." Against this background, Burton attempts to orient the vast prose poem which, in terms of originality and drama, has few equals among the literature of the world.

It has been suggested that some of the earliest parts of the Arabian Nights may date from the 8th century A.D., and that additions were made as late as the 16th century. There is some evidence that, as a collection, the work took on its present form about the 13th century, and that the addition of supplementary material did not alter the general pattern. Some of the thematic elements are probably of Far Eastern origin. The principal types of narrations combined to form the stories are animal fables, fairy tales, and historical, pseudo-historical, and traditional anecdotes.

The popular belief that the stories contained in the *Thousand and One Nights* belongs to a "tavern-literature," or were treasured only by the less privileged classes of Moslem society, is obviously untenable. It might as well be said that the Shakespearean plays were only appreciated or understood by the rustics frequenting the Globe Theater. The morality of both productions has been subject to some question, but in the case of the Arabian Nights, the natural disposition of the people, and the prevailing customs of their day, must be considered. Noble sentiments are frequently expressed, and the stories are permeated with the peculiar doctrines of mystical sects, and that broad transcendentalism which has always intrigued the Moslem mind.

For those willing to suspect that the Arabian Nights stories are more significant than at first appears, it is evident that many of the tales have double meanings, and when properly understood, are cleansed of all profane elements. As the studious mind has failed to solve the mystery of authorship, and even to identify those responsible for editorial policy, it may not be amiss to suspect that these relevant facts have been intentionally concealed. By a happy coincidence, the approximate dating for the original stories corresponds closely to the founding of the House of Wisdom in Cairo, and the broad program for the dissemination of philosophical knowledge which spread through Arabia and North Africa between the Ninth and Twelfth Centuries of the Christian era. The Greeks found much of philosophical importance in the writings of Homer, and when the *Odyssey* is compared with the journeys of Sinbad, the Sailor, one finds numerous parallels of meaning, and the ingenious use of esoteric symbolism. The same has been claimed for Virgil's *Ennead,* and today it would certainly be little better than a public proclamation of ignorance to deny that works like *Don Quixote de la Mancha* and *Gulliver's Travels* contain profound ideas cunningly concealed under extravagant fantasy. The works above mentioned have all been associated rather closely with secret societies functioning beneath the surface of European thinking. While it may be true that the average Moslem has made no systematic effort to "decode" his literary epic, it has received considerable attention from Western thinkers, who have found therein numerous traces of a worldwide esoteric tradition. It is very probable that a few learned Dervishes possess the true keys to the stories, but as usual are not inclined to reveal their knowledge.

Edward W. Lane-Poole appends to his translation of the *Thousand and One Nights* a valuable and extensive collection of notes, many of which support, at least indirectly, the serious intent behind these stories. In one of his notes, Lane-Poole gives attention to the spiritual magic believed in and practiced by even modern Moslems. Lane-Poole feels that this spiritual magic constitutes a link between the followers of Islam and other ancient religious groups. The Moslems recognized two basic forms of magic: one, divine or good; and the other, satanic or evil. Of divine magic, Lane-Poole gives us some rather interesting notes. It is a subtle science studied by good men, only for good purposes. Perfection in this secret science consists in the knowing of the most great name of God. This ultimate knowledge is imparted to none but the

A magical figure held in wide veneration and regarded as a powerful talisman to attract friendship and affection, according to the Cabala of the Saracens. From *Oedipus Aegyptiacus* by *Athanasius Kircher*.

peculiar favorites of heaven. It was by virtue of this name which he caused to be engraved on his signet ring, that King Solomon subjected to his dominion elementary spirits, birds, and even the wind.

It is known beyond question that among the learned Moslems there was a magical science equivalent to the Cabalism of Jewish and Christian mystics. The Jesuit scholar, Kircher, in his *Oedipus Aegyptiacus,* devotes considerable space to the Arabic Cabala. According to him, all speculations dealing with magical, alchemical, and thermaturgical mysteries known or practiced in Europe, or descending from the classical world, existed also among the Moslems. The Islamic mystics employed mysterious combinations of numbers, strange arrangements of words unintelligible to the uninitiated, peculiar diagrams and figures. In the preparation of charms and talismans they used enchantments for benevolent purposes, and were remarkably skilled in the divinatory arts.

While it is certain that such practices and beliefs were not favored by the more orthodox followers of the Prophet, they have survived the centuries, and may therefore be said to be according to the mind of the faithful. Where such researches were carried on, certain reports or accounts were circulated among the believers, who held the practitioners of these secret sciences in the highest admiration and regard. Those versed in these cabalistic arts were accredited with the wisdom and skill associated with the Adepts of Europe and Asia. The Arabian Nights abounds with reports of superphysical powers, and the accounts of the elusive saints of Moslem tradition mingle with the reports of the hidden Holy Ones of Jewish and early Christian legends. If such legends gained favor with less enlightened Moslems, it could only mean that the belief in the miraculous powers of sanctified persons was generally acceptable.

*The Faithful Brethren*

About the year A.D. 950, a secret society gained prominence at Basra, a port now in Iraq, on the Persian Gulf. This learned fraternity has been variously known as The Brethren of Purity, or The Faithful Friends. These designations have arisen from the original name, *Ihwan Al-Safa*. Although essentially a scientific group, at a time when science embraced nearly all forms of knowledge, sacred or profane, there is some indication that the Faithful Brethren were prepared to attempt a political reformation based upon the universal dissemination of essential learning. According to K. K. Doberer, this society had four degrees of initiation, and the inner teachings were compiled by sages forming the inner circle of masters or teachers. It was the practice of this fraternity to conform outwardly with the orthodox tenets of Islam, but inwardly to gather a vast storehouse of essential knowledge which could lead to a complete and practical philosophy for living. The society had many adversaries among orthodox Musselmen, especially in Baghdad, and efforts were made to destroy the books and tracts of the Order. These endeavors, however, were not successful, and the writings of the Faithful Brethren reached Europe, where they exercised influence on the political aspects of alchemy.*

F. Sherwood Taylor gives a further account of the Faithful Brethren. According to him, this organization is said to have composed an encyclopedic collection of letters, and he notes that it is suspected that this society was responsible for the extensive group of writings attributed to the Arabic chemist-mystic Geber who flourished in the 8th century.† As a young man, Geber became the disciple of the sixth She'ite Imam, from whom he received instruction in the occult sciences, and it is believed that he later joined the Sufi order.

The Faithful Brethren of Basra have been of interest to several Masonic writers. They are mentioned by John Yarker in his work on secret societies which have influenced the descent of Masonic traditions.‡ According to Kenneth Mackenzie, in his *Royal Masonic Encyclopedia,* the Brothers of Purity appear to have been influenced by the Essenes, and to have taught similar principles. Later, their writings were much studied by the most learned Spanish Jews. They

---

\* See *The Goldmakers.*
† See *The Alchemists, Founders of Modern Chemistry.*
‡ See *The Arcane Schools.*

had forms of initiation and have come to be regarded as a kind of Freemasons, and are so mentioned by the distinguished scholar Moritz Steinschneider. Albert Mackey, in his *An Encyclopedia of Freemasonry*, quotes Steinschneider (*Jew. Lit.*), who describes the Faithful Brethren as, "The Freemasons of Bosra," and "A celebrated society of a kind of Freemasons."

In his introduction to the *Mesnevi* of Jalal-ud-din, James W. Redhouse makes an intriguing observation: "One day, it is said, the Prophet (Muhammad) recited to 'Ali' in private the secrets and mysteries of the 'Brethren of Sincerity' (who appear to be the 'Freemasons' of the Moslem dervish world), enjoining on him not to divulge them to any of the uninitiated, so that they should not be betrayed; also, to yield obedience to the rules of implicit submission." Were the Brethren of Sincerity the same as the Basra fraternity of the Brethren of Purity? And does this further imply that this Society existed at the time of the Prophet, who either belonged to it, or was influenced by its teachings?

According to the doctrines of the Faithful Brethren, the moral nature of man is influenced by four factors, constituting together what psychologists might call environmental pressure. These modifying forces are bodily structure, climatic circumstances, educational conditioning, and the influence of the stars. If all the good qualities latent in the human being are cultivated, the perfected person exhibits the attributes of Plato's philosopher-king and the truly wise man of the stoics. Although they flourished within the Islamic community, these Pure Ones of Basra seem to have considered Socrates and Christ as equal to, if not actually superior to, the Prophet Mohammed. The sect is described as practicing a mystical intellectualism, but this did not prevent them from developing an encyclopedic system blending Neo-Pythagorean and Neoplatonic metaphysical speculations with the increasingly popular logical method of Aristotle.

The principal writings of the Faithful Brethren consisted

of fifty-two treatises divided into four sections. The first section was devoted to the abstract and speculative sciences; the second, to the natural and human sciences; the third, to metaphysics and the constitution of the soul and its rational attributes; and the fourth, to God, the divine world, and the mysteries of worship. They acknowledged prophetical revelation, practiced austerities, and sought to attain union with the spiritual power or principle which permeated all creation.

Mention is made of Maslama al-Majriti, who flourished in the 11th century. He was a Moslem born in Spain, and gained wide recognition as an encyclopedist. He traveled into the East, bringing back to Madrid a collection of the writings of the Faithful Brethren. The library in Vienna contains a work of this author, entitled *The Perfection of the Sage,* which deals with magic squares, arithmetical formulas, and the construction of talismans. From what little can be gathered, it appears reasonably certain that the Faithful Brethren represented a nucleus of universal scholarship involving both Eastern and Western doctrines, and not entirely limited to the Islamic world. Several writers who gained distinction in Europe during the medieval period, were influenced by the encyclopedic pattern advanced by the Brothers of Purity.

Among early European philosophers, scientists, and theologians who came under Moslem influence through contact with Spain, were Michael Scott and Roger Bacon. Scott (1175?-1234?), a Scottish scholar and astrologer, traveled to Toledo in order to gain a knowledge of Arabic and the Moslem sciences. While still at Oxford, Roger Bacon (1214?-1294), English friar-philosopher, achieved brilliant success as an exponent of Arabian Aristotelianism. Roger Bacon's work *Optics* was based on el Hazan's *Theosaurus Optica.* The works of Albertus Magnus, Vincent of Bovay, and Robert of England, all show indebtedness to the concepts outlined by the Faithful Brethren. It should be remembered that Christian Rosenkreutz, mysterious founder of the Rosicrucians, was said to have compiled an encyclopedia of universal knowledge while in the Near East, and that, returning to Europe, he stopped first in Spain to promulgate his doctrine. This may be a veiled reference to a motion of scholarship which has historical validity.

## The Cult of the Angel Peacock

The Yezidis are a small religious sect of uncertain origin, dwelling in the neighborhood of Mosul on the Tigris River in Northern Iraq, near the ruins of ancient Ninevah. In the 15th century, the Yezidis numbered approximately two hundred and fifty thousand. Since that time they have been subjected to many persecutions, and the membership has dwindled to not more than fifty thousand. The basic faith of these people is derived from early contacts with the numerous streams of religious tradition that have flowed through the valley of the Euphrates.

Isya Joseph, who made an extensive survey of the sacred books and traditions of the Yezidis, writes: "They say they have taken fasting and sacrifice from Islam; baptism from Christians; prohibition of foods from the Jews; their way of worship from the idolators; dissimulation of doctrine from the Rafidis (Shi'ites); human sacrifice and transmigration from the pre-Islamic paganism of the Arabs and from the Sabians." *

Although most historians and writers of fiction have assumed that the Yezidis were devil worshipers, the sacred writings and oral teachings of the sect do not sustain this assumption. A minority group of this kind, surrounded by powerful religions, whose doctrines they refused to accept, naturally was regarded with intense disfavor.

---

* *Devil Worship.*

In the Yezidi theology, the supreme deity, who was the first cause of the world, created the universe and then entrusted it to the keeping of seven gods, each of whom rules for ten thousand years. The present regent is Melek Ta-us. When his age or time is complete, the authority will pass to the next deity in the divine order. In the *Al-Jilway,* a sacred writing of the Yezidis, Melek Ta-us speaks through one of his prophets: "I am ever present to help all who trust in me and call upon me in time of need. There is no place in the universe that knows not my presence. I participate in all the affairs which those who are without (outsiders) call evil because their nature is not such as they approve. Every age has its own manager, who directs affairs according to my decrees. This office is changeable from generation to generation, that the ruler of this world and his chiefs may discharge the duties of their respective offices everyone in his own term."

Although the enemies of the sect insist that Melek Ta-us is the chief of the Fallen Angels, this is inconsistent with the basic concept which affirms seven gods to be the appointed representatives of the sovereign power that ordains all things in nature. Here we are certainly in the presence of Asiatic esotericism, and Melek Ta-us is the lord of the material world, and therefore the custodian of souls that have fallen into a state of generation.

The Yezidis venerate Melek Ta-us under a peculiar symbol which they call the *sanjak*. This is the figure of a peacock, described with a swelling breast, diminutive head, and wide-spread tail. Commonly made of brass, and crudely formed, this bird stands upon a base resembling a tall slender candlestick. In the religious ceremonies, two lamps with seven burners are associated with the central device. There are reports that magnificent forms of the peacock symbol, fashioned of pure gold and encrusted with gems, exist, but these have not been seen except by members of the Order.

Originally there were seven of the sacred *sanjaks,* one of which presided over each of the seven districts of the Yezidi communion. Some of these images were captured — that is, stolen — by the Islamites, in an effort to repress the faith. But the Yezidis only smiled, explaining that the idols taken from them were merely copies and that the originals were in a secure place.

The Yezidis believe in transmigration and reincarnation. They teach that the souls of the virtuous are reborn in human bodies, but those who have sinned against the faith or the faithful may come back to this world in the forms of animals. They practice mystical rites and disciplines, and believe that Melek Ta-us can speak to them through the lips of sanctified persons. If the messages given at various times differ or conflict it is of no consequence.

In the *Black Book* of the Yezidis, it is stated that the *sanjaks* were fashioned originally by one of the seven gods, who gave them into the keeping of Solomon the King. In the same work, it is stated definitely that Melek Ta-us descended to the earth in a remote time, dwelt with men and delivered to them his doctrines, rules, and traditions. The laws which he bestowed became a sacred heritage, and were passed down from generation to generation. There is constant insistence that the books and traditions of the Order shall be concealed from all unbelievers, lest the texts be perverted and the mysteries profaned.

In the period between November, 1845, and April, 1847, Mr. Austen Henry Layard, D.C.L., carried on extensive excavations at Nimrod. While at this site, he made several excursions into adjacent regions. He visited the mountain retreats of the Nestorians, and was privileged to attend the important yearly festival of the Yezidis. The details of his adventures are set forth in his book, *Nineveh and Its Remains*. Mr. Layard was especially successful in establishing the most friendly relations between himself and the native peoples, and was therefore permitted to be present at rites and ceremonies not usually accessible to foreigners. His summary of the Yezidi community is therefore of the greatest interest to scholars, as his information was secured first-hand, and he was able to make numerous discreet inquiries among leaders of the sect.

It was Layard's opinion that the mysteries of the sect can be traced to a form of worship introduced by Semiramis, Queen of Babylon, but he is convinced that the modern Yezidis practice none of the debased rites associated with the Babylonian cult. He found them a quiet and moral people of inoffensive demeanor and most kindly disposition. The rituals which Layard saw, though animated and including ceremonial dancing, were all of the most moral kind. He insists that no acts such as the Jewish law had declared to be impure are permitted. Layard testified that the Yezidis recognize one Supreme Being, but did not appear to offer any direct prayer or sacrifice to him. They especially feared the power of the Fallen Angel. Layard writes: "The name of the Evil spirit is, however, never mentioned; and any allusion to it by others so vexes and irritates them, that it is said they have put to death persons who have wantonly outraged their feelings by its use. So far is their dread of offending the Evil principle carried, that they carefully avoid every expression which may resemble in sound the name of Satan, or the Arabic word for 'accursed'."

According to Layard, when the Yezidis speak of the devil, they do so with reverence as Melek Ta-us, King Peacock, or Melek el Kout, the Mighty Angel. The Sheik Nasr admitted to him that they possessed a figure of a bird, but insisted that it be regarded as a symbol, and not as an idol. Without an adequate knowledge of the esoteric doctrine of the Yezidis, it is difficult to reconcile various accounts and reports, even if they be derived from members of the sect. According to Layard, "They believe Satan to be the chief of the Angelic host, now suffering punishment for his rebellion against the divine will; but still all-powerful, and to be restored hereafter to his high estate in the celestial hierarchy. He must be conciliated and reverenced, they say; for as he now has the power of doing evil to mankind, so will he hereafter have the power of rewarding them."

From this it cannot actually be inferred that these people worship evil; rather, that they are disinclined to antagonize the Fallen Angel. They live virtuous and honorable lives, so that when Satan is redeemed and becomes reunited with the principle of good, they may then enjoy rewards appropriate to their conduct. The men of the deserts and the mountains have always been of practical mind. With other old religions, they share the conviction that it is not necessary to make offerings to the Good Principle because, by its very nature, it will not injure them. Rather, they are concerned with the hazards and dangers of living, personified as an adversary who must be appeased, lest he bring immediate calamity upon those who incur his enmity. Were they truly devil-worshipers, they would not have venerated Christ, who to them was a great angel who had taken the form of man. If we understand by their concept of Satan the "Prince of this World," referred to in the New Testament, who is to govern the interval between the fall of man and his redemption, and interpret this in the experience of a simple and isolated group, the apparent conflict of ideas becomes comprehensible, if not entirely consistent.

The Yezidis hold the Old Testament in great reverence, believing in the cosmogony of Genesis, the Deluge, and other Biblical events. They do not reject either the New Testament or the Koran; they look upon Mohammed as a prophet, and also venerate Abraham and the other patriarchs. They look to a second coming of Christ, and also expect the reappearance of the Imam Mahdi. The Sheik Adi is regarded as their great saint, but Layard was unable to learn any particulars concerning him. Even his date of existence is uncertain, and the Sheik Nasr asserted that he lived before Mohammed. This Sheik Adi had communion with celestial personages and performed miracles. Legendry suggests that he might be included among Near Eastern Adepts. Layard also suspected that from their chronology, the Yezidis might have been connected with the cult of Manes. At the time Layard attended their ceremonies, they chanted an ancient melody, a part of which was called the Song of the Angel Jesus. The language was so corrupt, however, that the words were unintelligible.

All this symbolism is part of the usual paraphernalia of a lodge of initiates or adept-teachers. The seven brazen peacocks stand for the masters of the Yezidis, and behind the outer form of the sect is a secret doctrine of ideas. The persecutions through which they have passed have caused the Yezidis to protect their esoteric cult in every way possible. It is extremely doubtful if any non-Yezidi understands the mystery of the Dark Star with its brooding regent. Occasionally, some fragment of this old wisdom-religion comes to light, but for the most part, the secrets are reserved for those who have solved the mystery of the Angel Peacock.

*The Druses of the Lebanon*

In the mystical sect of the Druses, several streams of highly specialized and extremely profound religious teachings, both Eastern and Western, have been imposed upon a people neither profoundly learned nor especially suitable to become so. Today the sect numbers approximately one hundred fifty thousand, and is scattered through the smaller communities of Syria and contiguous areas. The Druses follow a system involving elements of the Orphic mysticism of the Greeks, Indian esotericism, Near Eastern and North African transcendentalism, Old Testament moralism, Islamic ethical speculations, star worship, and the Avestic literature of Persia. Obviously, such ingredients are incomprehensible to the average Druse, who is satisfied to believe that his faith is predestined to unite the religions of the world and to end forever those fanatical tendencies which have from time immemorial, divided the devout.

Even the simple and natural desire to reconcile men of good spirit contributed to the misfortunes which have plagued the Druses for centuries. Tolerance has never been popular, and the sects and creeds flourishing in the regions occupied by the Druse communities have slight sympathy for the votaries of this strange faith. The Christians resent the Moslem sympathies of the group, and the Moslems are suspicious of the Christian and Jewish content in the Druse doctrines. Altogether this minority cult is between the upper and lower grindstone, and has survived precariously for centuries. Nor have the Druses become more popular as the result of proclaiming their special interest in the moral and ethical culture of China. They feel that the Chinese are Druses by conviction, if not by name.

To escape the persecution of powerful neighbors, the Druses have incorporated into their code an article of faith which permits them to conceal their membership in the Order and to proclaim themselves orthodox members of any faith dominant in the area where they live. Thus they live in a state of public conformity and private dissension. They further justify their attitude on the grounds that all other religions are corrupt forms of Drusedom. Fortunately, they are not inclined to proselyte, and have no interest in making converts, and this disinterestedness has prevented their extinction. Although it is usual to consider them as an offshoot of Islamism, it is doubtful if that assumption is correct. The sect arose among the Moslems, but from the beginning, exhibited characteristics suggesting Gnosticism. The Gnostics flourished in North Africa, where Drusedom was born, and it might be more accurate to trace the sect to the revival of classical philosophy among the Moslems. Just as Mohammed himself was strongly influenced by Nestorian Christianity and Judaism, the founders of the Druse sect were evidently acquainted with several philosophical systems. The Drusean attitude toward the complex problem of the man Jesus and the Christ principle, is certainly based upon the teachings of the Alexandrian Gnostics.

The Druses have an excellent reputation for thrift, hospitality, and courage. They will converse freely on almost any subject except the secrets of their religion. If pressed too far, they may have a convenient lapse of memory or experience unusual difficulties with language. Like most devout peoples, however, they have a keen sense for estimating human nature, and a few non-Druses who showed an honest desire for knowledge, and appropriate capacities of temperament, have been permitted to learn some parts of the Drusean doctrine. By living quietly in a community of Druses and gradually gaining the respect of the sect, it is possible to overcome slowly the reticence of these people.

According to history, Drusedom was founded in the 11th century of the Christian era by Ismail Ad-darazi, a Persian mystic. At that time, Al-hakim bi'amrillahi was the Fatimid Caliph of Egypt. Under the pressure of a rising mystical conviction, this Caliph proclaimed himself to be an incarnation of God, and being apparently of unsound mind, he reigned erratically and despotically until his final disappearance in A.D. 1021. It seems probable that he was assassinated, but, as his fate was never clearly established, curious legends gained wide circulation. Actually, Al-hakim was little more than a name, and it cannot be assumed that he originated the doctrines associated with him. The Druses of the Lebanon have been falsely accused of deriving their religion from a mad Caliph, whose temperament was reminiscent to that of Nero. Actually, both Moslem and non-Moslem Druses follow an elevated moral and ethical code which causes them to be considered more or less puritanical by neighboring unbelievers.

There are a number of Druses in the United States, but they usually pass as Syrian Christians and are not likely to discuss their faith unless the listener is informed and sympathetic. There is nothing in the manner or attitude of the educated Druse to suggest that his background is in any way remarkable. In business he is honorable; in his private life, kindly and tolerant; and in public matters, he exhibits a strong sense of civic responsibility. In discussing their religion with Syrian Druses who have become American citizens, it has been my experience that they regard many of their older beliefs as folklore, but are quickly responsive to references made to the esoteric doctrines of Oriental nations. One told me that he had heard from his mother about the existence of adepts and secret schools in remote Asia, but had not given the matter serious thought until he contacted mystical groups in America. Like the followers of most other faiths the Druses are receptive to the idea of a secret doctrine concealed beneath the outer forms of religious systems. As one expressed it: "I was told these things when a child, but I did not understand."

The Drusean system of initiation, like that of most esoteric sects, includes visions, trances, and related psychic phenomena. The Masters of the sect are undoubtedly well trained in natural magic and, like the priests of most ancient sects, are able to cause miraculous occurrences. Perhaps their disciplines were derived from the Ophites, who were skilled in secret arts. Certainly the higher members of the Drusean sect are so convinced of the validity of their esoteric sciences that they cannot be converted to any other faith. Their rites include fasting, rituals of purification, and obligations of secrecy. They also share in the concept of many fraternities, as these relate to mutual aid, to the protection of members, and to the performance of charity.

The Druses have seven commandments, or tenets, which they obey and practice: 1) God is one and indivisible. 2) Truth is supreme. 3) Religious tolerance is a virtue. 4) All men and women of good character are entitled to respect. 5) Complete obedience to the decrees of God. 6) Purity of mind, soul, and body. 7) Mutual help and support in time of need.

Both men and women are eligible for initiation on terms of complete equality. This in itself is unusual among Eastern sects. Masters of the Drusean faith are regarded as exceedingly venerable and are consulted on important matters. Their advice or opinion is usually followed without question. Children are well treated in the Drusean community, and the family life is simple and dignified. In older times, education was largely in the keeping of advanced members of the group. Though not especially warlike, the Druses are ready to defend their culture, and there have been periods of intense strife between them and the Moslem groups. Most of these difficulties, however, belong to the past, and today the communities are peaceful and industrious.

It is not easy to summarize the doctrine of the Druses. Most available information is derived from antagonistic sources, either Christian or Moslem. Even those who desired to be fair have either lacked direct contact with the sect or have been influenced to some degree by popular reports. The summary given by the Earl of Carnarvon is about the best available: "The imposing doctrine of faith in one God, in whom there are no parts, to whom no attributes can be assigned, before whom the tongue refuses to utter, the eye to see, the mind to understand, whose very name is ineffable, which crowns the pyramid of Druse theology, might seem to remove Heaven too far from men and their affairs; and therefore the weaknesses of human nature have been well accommodated by the reflexion and incarnation of the Deity in successive ages. Nine times previously in India, Arabia, Persia, and Africa—so Hamze taught—had the Supreme Intelligence deigned to reveal himself under the form and name of mortal men. In the person of Hakem, for the tenth and last time, God's will was republished, His forbearance manifested, and a final appeal made to the obduracy of the world. For twenty-six years 'the door,' in the figurative language of the Druse doctors, stood open to Christian or Mahommedan, Jew or Gentile; but when that term of grace had expired, the work of conversion was closed, and the world was left uninvited and unenlightened for the future, till in the great consummation of mortal things, amid the gathering of armies and tribulations of the faithful, when Mahommedanism shall fail and Mecca be no longer sacred, Hakem shall reappear to conquer the earth and to give supremacy to the Druse religion."

Missionaries who have attempted to penetrate into the secret rites of the Druses have occasionally been permitted to witness ceremonials manufactured for the entertainment of persistent unbelievers. This has led to the conclusion that Drusedom consists of two conflicting systems of doctrine— one for the laity, and another for the initiated. Actually, the esoteric content is merely an extension of the exoteric tradition, whereby, through interpretation, mysterious realities are first sensed and finally known.

Another quotation from the Earl of Carnarvon, who "passed through the region," conveys the bewilderment of the Occidental: "Gradually—very gradually—he (the neophyte) is permitted to draw aside the successive veils which shroud the great secret: he perceives the deep meaning of numbers, he understands the dark sayings in which the sacred writings, that he has hitherto accepted in their literal sense, convey in doubtful phrase a double and a different meaning to the ear and the mind. The Koran becomes an allegory; the life and actions even of his own Immam are but the shadows of distant truths; . . . . Still, as he presses on, he perceives that he is unravelling the web that he had just woven—that he is learning only to unlearn; he makes, and he treads on the ruins of his former beliefs; slowly, painfully, dizzily, he mounts each successive degree of initiation, until the mystical seven, or the not less mystical nine, are accomplished, and—as if to mock the hope of all return—at each stride he hears the step on which he last trod crumble and crash into the measureless abyss that rolls below him."†

Lord Carnarvon's description is dramatic, if not completely factual. The Western mind is not conditioned for

---

\* *Recollections of the Druses of the Lebanon* (London, 1860).
† Ibid.

cabalistic speculation. To the literal theologian, the possibility of a secret faith which can bestow an inner illumination and transform the material substances of a belief through inspiration and revelation seems little more than a fantastic superstition. Even after a Druse teacher has emphasized the importance of the allegorical key to his faith, the outsider seldom applies this key to the fables which the Druse patiently unfolds. Would it be likely that the members of a mystical sect, the Masters of which have been enlightened by meditation, prayer, and lives of piety, could literally believe that the unsavory Caliph Al-hakim was actually the incarnation of God, or that the door of salvation stood open for only twenty-six years?

In all probability, the legends of the Druses must be approached with the same attitude with which one should examine the mythology of the Grecians. Only by acknowledging the existence of a profound language of symbolism can the conduct of the Olympian deities be reconciled with the lofty convictions of Pythagoras and Plato. The Greek philosophers, scientists, mathematicians, and legislators would not have acknowledged the divine authority of an order of divinities whose characteristics were less heavenly than the manners of the decadent Athenian aristocracy. The *Encyclopedia Britannica* acknowledges that the sacred books of the Druse religion "contain moral teachings of a high order on the whole."

The Druses consider both the Christian Gospels and the Koran to be inspired writings, but only the Druse Scriptures are accepted as correct guides to spiritual conduct. All other religions, by allegorical interpretation, are made to support the Drusean revelation. Here is a broad application of the Neoplatonic concept that all religions and philosophies are identical, when unlocked by the proper key. Mystics, regardless of their affiliations, pass through the same experiences when they apply the principles of internal growth. Although the Druses do not require ascetic practices, their beliefs lead inevitably toward detachment from materialistic interests and pursuits. The Drusean mystics share the attitudes of unworldliness which distinguish the more advanced Dervishes and Sufis.

The sect believes in reincarnation, and holds that each embodiment is nobler than the previous one. The process of rebirth continues until the mystical resurrection. The physical body, with its lower mental and emotional attributes, is the enemy of man's spiritual purpose. There are elements of anthropomorphism similar to those in the Mazdian cult, where powers of light and darkness struggle for domination over the human destiny. Security against evil is attained by obedience to the Drusean code, which was given by God, through His embodiments, for the preservation of His creatures. The neophyte must learn the false doctrines of the world, in order to receive into his heart the secret of the mystery of life. This process of unlearning becomes increasingly severe as the disciple advances through the grades of the sect. He is struggling against illusion, and in so doing, must overcome his own mind and accept without reservation the impression of the divine purpose.

Lord Carnarvon's description of the neophyte treading on the ruins of his former beliefs would be the natural reaction of the uninitiated. True humility is complete submission to the Divine Will. To overcome the world, the neophyte must overcome the worldliness in himself. Not only the shadow (materialism), but also the works of the shadow must be conquered. To the Druse, the works of the shadow include even the human attitude toward God, religion, and philosophy. He has been accused of choosing a path which leads, in the end, to a monstrous unbelief. The simplest explanation of his faith is to compare it with Buddhism and the Buddhistic concept of Nirvana. To the Christian, the Nirvana is simply total extinction of self, an idea frightening and repulsive to the average believer.

The Druse resurrection is the re-identification of the spirit in man with the universal spirit, which is all-pervading. This is not extinction, but universalization. The one does not become nothing; it becomes all. Certainly it is impossible for mortal man to know, as inward fact, an unlimited condition of consciousness. The Druse system gradually enlarges and impersonalizes the spiritual convictions of the individual, until the ideal of universalization becomes not only attractive, but also completely satisfying. To awake from the illusion of diversity to the realization of unity is the fulfillment of man's supreme destiny. Just as the word *yoga* means *union*, the Druse prefers to be called a unifier. He strengthens his resolutions by the constant discovery and experience of unity. He sees the religions of the world gradually awaking to the awareness of unity. He contemplates the coming together of nations and the gathering of knowledge by emphasis upon common denominators. With the aid of allegory and interpretation, he is able to perceive those eternal verities enthroned behind the shadowy and illusional divisions which have so long prevented men from laboring together in common causes.

From the earliest time, God has sent His teachers and His prophets to reveal His will and to purify doctrines corrupted by human ignorance. Mankind has not the strength or courage to practice or preserve the Divine wisdom, and the revelations brought by the anointed messengers were perverted through selfishness and ignorance. To prevent doctrinal errors from frustrating the spiritual aspirations of humanity, reformers came to purify earlier revelations and to restore the essential principles of religion. In the Druse system, one hundred and sixty-four great teachers are enumerated, and because of their mighty efforts, there has never been a time when the world has been without spiritual guidance. There is the implication that all the teachers brought one essential doctrine, although they appeared in different places and their revelations received various names.

In addition to these messengers, the Deity itself became peculiarly and particularly embodied in ten Messiahs, who correspond with the Avatars of Vishnu in the Hindu system. The prophet Hamsa was the precursor of the tenth Avatar of the Druses. Like John the Baptist, he announced the coming of Al-hakim. More mystically speaking, Hamsa represented Jesus, and Al-hakim the Christ. Obviously, the mystical tradition is not actually concerned with personalities at all, and the effort to associate universal principles with historical personages has resulted in serious misunderstandings. Hamsa, in a way, personifies the Druse Adept, who, having advanced to the highest state of personal sanctity, has become a vessel capable of receiving into itself the Divine incarnation.

In the Druse communities, places of initiation are set aside for the performance of the rites and ceremonies. These chambers are undergound and, with the exception of certain celebrated sanctuaries, have only the simplest of furnishings. The prayer rug can be symbolical of the chamber of initiation. The room merely represents a state of aloofness from material concerns. It is not essentially a place, but a condition of consciousness. The initiation rituals follow closely the rites of Greece and Egypt. The candidate is tested by trials of physical strength and endurance, moral temptations, and is further examined for his aptitude in the learning and disciplines of the sect. Very few are able to pass all the tests successfully, but those whose ability and character are worthy of consideration may wait a year and try again. The severity of the physical ordeals accounts for many failures, but there are indications that these tests are not so severe now as in earlier times. Those who pass the examination successfully are accepted into the inner sanctuary of the Order, and are given signs of recognition and further instruction in the esoteric sciences.\*

Referring to the initiation rites of the Druses, Mme. Blavatsky points out that on certain occasions, a solemn ceremony takes place during which the initiates of the higher

---

\* For details concerning initiation into the Druse sect, see the letter by Professor A. L. Rawson, describing his own initiation, in *Isis Unveiled*, by H. P. Blavatsky.

degrees start out on pilgrimage into certain hidden places in the mountains. She writes: "They meet within the safe precincts of a monastery said to have been erected during the earliest times of the Christian era. Outwardly one sees but old ruins of a once grand edifice, used, says the legend, by some Gnostic sect as a place of worship during the religious persecution. The ruins above ground, however, are but a convenient mask; the subterranean chapel, halls, and cells, covering an area of ground far greater than the upper building; while the richness of ornamentation, the beauty of the ancient sculptures, and the gold and silver vessels in this sacred resort, appear like 'a dream of glory' according to the expression of an initiate."*

Although seldom mentioned in the accounts of this sect, there is evidence that the Druses acknowledge the existence of an association of Adepts and Masters, who form a superior council. These illumined teachers, like the fabled Mahatmas of India, are extremely elusive, but may appear when the need arises. They are known by their wonderful powers and remarkable sanctity, but their comings and goings are inexplicable. Some of the more venerable Druse doctors are believed to have contact with these immortal-mortals, who alone are perfect in the doctrine. In the areas where the Druses flourish, legends and reports about these Adepts are quietly circulated. They are seldom, if ever, mentioned to strangers.

It is quite possible that American Druses and more enlightened members in the Near Eastern communities could be induced to prepare a reasonably correct account of the sect and its doctrine. Groups of this kind are concerned over the encroachment of modern materialism, and recognize the desirability of providing qualified persons with reliable information. The project languishes, however, because the sect is one of many minority groups about which there is no general concern. When we realize that the Near

---

* See *Isis Unveiled*, Vol. II.

Typical Dervishes belonging to Eastern Moslem communities.

## THE MYSTICS OF ISLAM 87

East has supplied the religious incentives to three great continents, and that nearly half the civilized world is influenced by doctrines originating in the area of the Lebanon, there should be more interest in uncovering the foundations of now-dominant faiths.

The effects of Drusedom upon Europe were considerable during the medieval period, and the modern world is still dominated religiously, politically, and culturally by medievalism. The Crusaders, especially the Knights Templars, the Knights of Malta, and the Teutonic Knights, contacted the Druses and were influenced by many of their doctrines. The direct result was the Renaissance, and among later consequences was the Reformation. Mystical interpretations of Christianity increased rapidly and broadened the foundations of the faith. It is believed that a number of the European Knights were actually initiated into the Syrian Mysteries and the Secret Orders of Islam.* Through them the great heresy reached Europe, supplying the impulse which ultimately overthrew spiritual, intellectual, and physical feudalism. "The constant intercourse between Syria and Europe, maintained first by the flocks of pilgrims perpetually crowding to Jerusalem, then by the Crusades, and lastly by the establishment of the Frankish kingdom in Palestine, and of the different principalities upon the coast, produced vast effects, both apparent and concealed, upon the nations of Europe, more especially those seated upon the Mediterranean."†

### The Dervish Fraternity

In western Asia, there are a number of mystical sects which have evolved from and within the faith of Islam. Among these, the Dervish Orders are the best known and

---
\* See Adler, *Drusis Montis Libani* (Rome, 1786).
† C. W. King, *The Gnostics and Their Remains*.

the most likely to be contacted by travelers and tourists. Within the Dervish Fraternity, there are twelve principal Orders, each governed by a chief to whom is given complete allegiance. The members are initiated by rites which appear to the uninformed to be barbaric and fantastic. The spiritual fraternities of the Dervishes are highly respected throughout the Moslem world. The attitude toward them is not so different from the esteem in which wandering bands of friars were held in Christendom of the Middle Ages. The Dervishes are regarded as persons possessing supernormal faculties, and are consulted in matters requiring extraordinary discernment.

Two general types of holy men are to be found in the mystical fraternities of Islam. The first is the scholarly and consecrated Dervish, whose life is devoted to the study of the secret spiritual forces of the universe. The second is the religious mendicant, who, for one reason or another, has renounced worldliness and lives by the generosity of the faithful. It is believed, however, that exalted souls may conceal their identities under most pitiful appearances; therefore, it is unwise to neglect the requirements of even the most lowly of the religious mendicants.

The Orders of Dervishes can be distinguished by the color and form of their garments and the number of folds in their turbans. The peculiar powers of the Dervishes have been attested by many Europeans, and the fakirs are famous for their skill in conjuration. Some of the Dervish sects are in more or less close association with Eastern Freemasonry and the Druses of Syria. The esoteric rites and practices of many Near Eastern sects belong to a common stream of tradition, a fact that is recognized by the better-informed members, even though the less enlightened cling to fanatical attitudes of isolation.

The outer or visible body of Dervishes consists of organizations or groups of disciples who study the mysteries of life from ancient and venerable teachers. Behind the visible structure of Dervish mysticism, however, is a secret invisible institution composed of illumined Masters, who only upon rare occasions contact disciples of the lower grades. This inner body of God-instructed men possesses the fullness of divine knowledge, and membership comes as the reward for outstanding achievement in the lower grades of the Brotherhood. L.M.J. Garnett writes of the Dervishes thus: "According to the mystical canon, there are always on earth a certain number of holy men who are admitted to intimate communion with the Deity."* J. P. Brown refers to these spiritual ones as the "Master Souls."† They are still in the physical body and wander about the earth, but are recognizable only by the elect. The Dervishes teach that any person whom they meet, even the poorest beggar, may be one of these Master souls.

At the head of the hierarchy composing the inner or mystical Dervish Order is a most august soul, who is called the "Axis" or "Pole" of the universe. His identity is unknown, even to the highest members of the Order, and he often wanders the earth in the garb of a novice. He is a Master of the power of magic, can make himself invisible at will, and traverse vast distances with the speed of thought. On either side of the "Axis" are two great souls subordinate only to himself. When the time comes for the "Axis" to leave his physical body and ascend into the sphere of light, then the "Faithful One" on his right is advanced to the dignity of Axis, and all the other members of the Order correspondingly advance one degree to fill the vacancies created. This great body of spiritual mystics, collectively the "Lords of Souls" and "Directors," is an invisible government controlling all the temporal institutions of Islam, and far surpassing in power all earthly monarchies. There is a considerable discussion of the hierarchy of Divine Friends (Walees), in the *Fawaed-i-Rukni* of Shaikh Sharfuddin Maneri.‡

---

\* *Mysticism and Magic in Turkey.*
† See *The Dervishes.*
‡ See *Letters from a Sufi Teacher,* translated by Baijnath Singh.

Dervishes performing their Cosmic Dance. From *Picart's Religious Ceremonials*.

With an outer organization of many thousands of Dervishes of varying degrees of holiness, and an inner body composed of God-men so highly advanced and so superior to ordinary humanity that they seem more mystical than real, it is evident that the Dervishes form a very powerful Order in the Islamic world. Each Dervish, it is said, is founded in the faith through having passed successfully a thousand and one days and nights of temptation. Renouncing everything pertaining to the flesh, these men have devoted their lives to the perfection of consciousness.

One of the most interesting sects of the Dervishes is the Order of Mevlevi, more commonly known as the dancing or whirling Dervishes, and popularly supposed to have been founded by the great Persian Sufi poet and philosopher, Jalal-ud-din Rumi (1207-1273). The astonishing ability of the whirling Dervish to spin with incredible velocity and then to stop suddenly to lean over and pick up a pin is amazing. He can continue this dancing motion for a considerable time, and no amount of spinning causes dizziness. From what can be gleaned in the fragmentary extracts from the doctrines which have come into the hands of the profane, the purpose of the whirling is to attune the rhythm of the body to the circular motion of the celestial spheres.

Like many religious Orders in various parts of the world, the Dervishes have strange practices intended to produce the ecstatic condition. In some cases, they even resort to the use of hashish to bring about a temporary clairvoyance, but this practice can hardly be considered representative of the true ideals of Dervishism.

The Mevlevis wear tall but not pointed caps, and their garments are tight about the waist, but flare out below, like an extremely full skirt, to the ankle. During the whirling dances, these skirts stand straight from the body in a large circle, making the Dervish resemble a spinning top. The various groups of Dervishes wear different styles of caps, all of which are more or less significant. One type of headgear is vase-shaped and symbolizes the urn of spiritual light in which God kept the soul of Mohammed before the birth of the Prophet.

There is another interesting point brought out, at least theoretically, in Dervish philosophy. Obeying the ancient custom of the Brotherhood, the various members of the Order always travel in certain directions of the compass and at certain angles. Consequently, if one desires to meet a certain Dervish saint, it is first necessary to learn the angle upon which he travels. If the seeker will then place himself at some point along the line of this angle, and await the Dervish, the latter will ultimately appear.

The Dervishes possess a secret doctrine concerning human regeneration which has many points of similarity with the mysticism of the Brahmans. Dervish philosophy may be summarized as the Oriental doctrine of realization. By renouncing human consciousness, and rising above all limitations of the sense perceptions and the intellect, the Dervish attains to a level of transcendent understanding in which he feels himself absorbed into the nature of the Universal Being. The Dervish neophyte advances along "paths." These paths, or degrees, are four in number, and each is governed by a personification of a divine attribute. In the first degree, the novice seeks absorption in the Sheik, or Master, of the path. In the second degree, the disciple aspires to identification with the illustrious sage who founded the discipline, or path. In the third degree, the initiate attempts to accomplish absorption into the Prophet Mohammed; and in the fourth degree, the Adept seeks complete universalization in Deity.

John P. Brown, whose text *The Dervishes* is still one of the principal reference works on the subject, derives the word *Dervish* from two Persian syllables, the first meaning *a door,* and the second, *to beg.* It is questionable, however, if the term actually means *to beg from door to door.* More likely it signifies those who ask alms at the door of truth. Originally, the Islamic mystics were small groups of disciples who accepted without question the spiritual leadership of some enlightened saint or distinguished teacher. Mystics have never been conformists, and have always depended upon direct extrasensory experience for inspiration and guidance. Like the philosophical schools which flourished in the Golden Age of Greek learning, the size and distinction of a sect depended largely upon the fame and accomplishments of the leader. A few outstanding teachers, like Pythagoras and Plato, left behind them such strongly integrated associations that these survived and became enduring organizations. Leadership passed to elder disciples who, in turn, selected their successors, thus establishing a lasting pattern of descent.

This is in essence the story of the Dervish Orders, and, because their mysticism was associated with the traditions, rites, and ceremonies of the Moslems, they belong with this religion. Actually, however, their mysticism transcends all sectarian limitation, and their illuminations confer upon them a universal citizenship. Although the Dervishes are regarded as the principal monastic order of the Islamic world, they differ from Christian monastic groups in one particular: They give no allegiance to the orthodox faith and receive no benefits therefrom. They survive entirely by their own efforts, and enjoy the privilege of administering their affairs as they see fit. The Dervishes receive considerable public support, and it is considered injudicious to deny them any reasonable request. Although critics insist that these Orders survive upon the gullibility of the ignorant, this is not strictly true. We may as well say that all religions depend for their existence upon the generosity of the faithful. The Dervish influence is so widespread that in some areas every Mussulman is to some degree asssociated with one of the several Orders. There are instances in which tradesmen and merchants constitute Dervish guilds.

Many authors refer to the similarities between the Dervishes and European Freemasons. For example, Brown notes that ". . . . the Dervishes of the Bektashee Order consider themselves quite the same as the Freemasons, and are disposed to fraternize with them."* Probably the analogies are due to parallels of doctrine and ritual. As early European Freemasonry was strongly influenced by Near Eastern sects, and its roots were deep in the symbolism of old Orders which flourished in Syria and Arabia, there are vestiges of Oriental mysticism in Western Masonry. Today, however, the Dervish remains essentially a mystical philosopher, and as such, will have conflict with the prevailing tendency to ignore the esoteric content of rituals and symbols.

---

* *The Dervishes.*

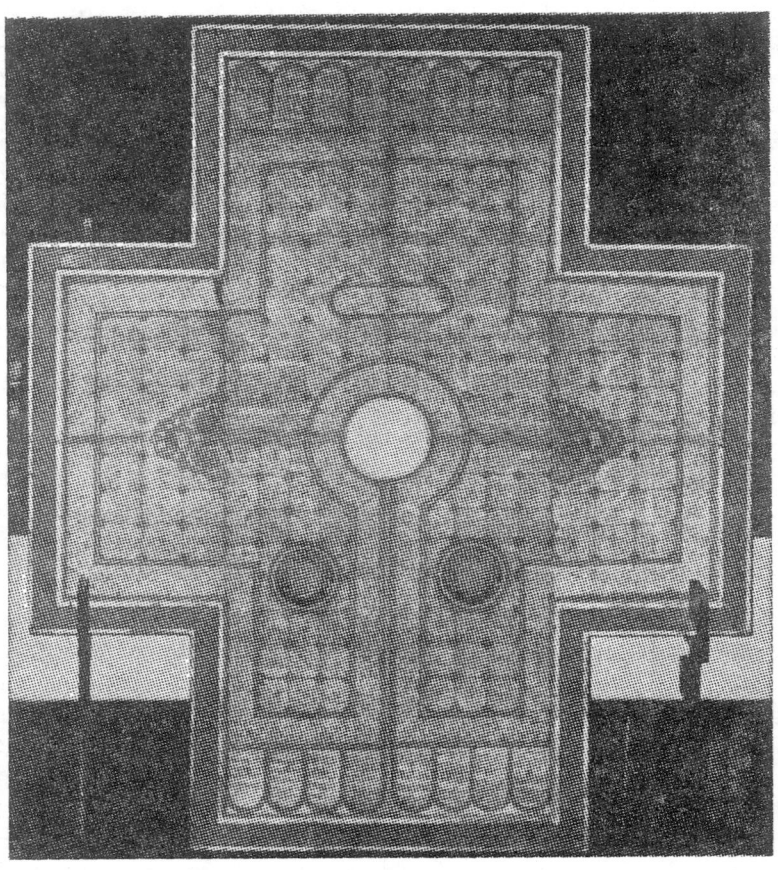

A cope in the shape of a Cross. A religious cape with large sections of the Koran on its panels—painted—in pinkish red color and worn by some pious Pilgrim on his journey to Mecca.

On a few occasions, the Dervishes have been involved in the political ambitions of Islamic leaders. Such pressures have affected adversely most religious groups, but should not be regarded as representative of the real convictions of monastic orders. After all, the Dervish Orders have become so diffused throughout the life of the Islamic people that the conduct of individual members or even groups does not indicate the temper of the more enlightened mystic. Fanaticism is present in all religious communities and has brought discredit upon many worthy and commendable organizations. By his own creed and doctrine, the Dervish is a man of peace, dedicated to charitable works and the attainment of internal tranquility. All to the contrary results from abuse or misunderstanding of principles.

Wherever men feel that they have received Divine insight, the prophetic spirit produces various forms of divination. Some Dervishes have become famous for reading human destiny in sand, by the stars, or by gazing upon magical objects. There is wide belief in omens and portents, and, while some of these soothsayers are of doubtful ability, the majority are obviously sincere, if not entirely proficient. Certain Dervishes have made remarkable prophecies which have been fully justified by subsequent facts. The Dervish Orders are especially interesting because they form an impressive unit within the world concept of mysticism. They supply further evidence of the existence of an esoteric tradition concerning the possibility of the human being advancing his internal life by meditative disciplines.

## *Jalal-ud-din Rumi, the Great Dervish Adept*

In his introduction to the Mesnevi of Jalal-ud-din, James W. Redhouse states that about A.D. 1260, Jalal-ud-din was urged by Hasan Husam al-din to compose the *Mesnevi*. Scholars in the field are inclined to consider this work, which is divided into six books, as the greatest mystical poem ever written. The Preface opens with the following statement: "This is the book of the Rhymed Couplets (Mathnawi, Mesnevi). It contains the roots of the roots of the roots of the (one true) Religion (of Islam); and treats of the discovery of the mysteries of reunion and sure knowledge. It is the Grand Jurisprudence of God, the most glorious Law of the Deity, the most manifest Evidence of the Divine Being. The refulgence thereof 'is like that of a lantern in which is a lamp' that scatters beams more bright than the morn. It is the paradise of the heart, with springs and foliage." The inner quote in this passage is from the Koran. In presenting this work to the English reader, Redhouse, by way of introduction, gives selected anecdotes from Menaqibu 'L 'Arifin, The Acts of the Adepts, by Shemsu-'D-Din Ahmed, El Eflaki. This work is concerned with accounts of the miraculous lives of Moslem saints and sages, and includes a section devoted to incidents in the career of Jalal-ud-din Rumi. It is from this section that the following episodes relating to Jalal-ud-din are derived.

Jalal-ud-din, the great Dervish Adept, was born on the 29th of September, A.D. 1207. When only five years old, this remarkable man became strangely and profoundly agitated by a series of extraordinary occurrences. "The cause of these perturbations was that spiritual forms and shapes of the absent (invisible world) would arise before his sight, that is, angelic messengers, righteous genii, and saintly men —the concealed ones of the bowers of the True One (spiritual spouses of God), used to appear to him in bodily shape, exactly as the cherubim and seraphim used to show themselves to the holy apostle of God, Muhammed, in the earlier days, before his call to the prophetic office; as Gabriel appeared to Mary, and as the four angels were seen by Abraham and Lot; as well as others to other prophets."

When Jalal-ud-din was about six years old, he received a further mystical experience. While frolicking with several other children, he suddenly disappeared from among his playmates, causing them great consternation. Later he explained that while he had been speaking with his friends, "a company of visible forms, clad in green raiment, had led him away from them, and had conducted him about the various concentric orbs of the spheres, and through the signs of the Zodiac, showing him the wonders of the world of spirits, and bringing him back to them as soon as their cries had reached his ears."

Two years after the death of his father, Jalal-ud-din having reached his 23rd year, journeyed to Aleppo to advance his learning. While in this city, he excited the jealousy and suspicion of some of his fellow students, who complained to the governor that this extraordinary young man left his cell at midnight each night for some mysterious purpose which they suspected might be immoral. The governor, possessed by typical Oriental curiosity, decided to discover the truth for himself. He therefore hid where he could watch Jalal-ud-din from a safe distance. Exactly at low twelve, the locked gate of the college opened of itself, and Jalal-ud-din came forth. He then passed through the great gate of the city which also opened without human hands. The governor, attempting to follow, felt himself moving at incredible speed for a considerable distance. The trip ended at the tomb of Abraham at Hebron, nearly three hundred and fifty miles from Aleppo. The governor then beheld a domed edifice, wherein was congregated a large company of mysterious beings wearing green robes, who came forth to meet Jalal-ud-din. They embraced him with affection and then conducted him into the building. The governor became so frightened that he fainted. When he awoke, the domed building was gone, and the bewildered magistrate was hopelessly lost in the desert. Two days later he was found and brought home in an exhausted condition. Naturally, he decided not to pursue the subject any further.

Eastern literature abounds with remarkable accounts of miraculous occurrences involving Jalal-ud-din. During his last illness, a friend was seated by him. Suddenly a most handsome youth appeared at the door of the room. Jalal-ud-din immediately arose, and advanced to receive the stranger, who said, "I am 'Azra'il the angel of departure and separation. I come, by the Divine command to inquire what commission the Master may have to entrust to me." The Dervish Adept replied, "Come in, come in, thou messenger of my King. Do that which thou art bidden; and, God willing, thou shalt find me one of the patient."

Perhaps the most significant story about the mysterious hierarchy of Adepts was told by the widow of Jalal-ud-din, who was regarded as a model of virtue. She related what she had seen through a chink in the door, where her husband and one of his associates were closeted in spiritual communion. Suddenly the wall of the room opened and six men of majestic mien entered through the cleft. These strangers, who were of the occult saints, saluted, bowed, and laid a nosegay of bright flowers at the feet of Jalal-ud-din, although it was then in the depth of the midwinter season. They remained until the hour of sunrise worship. When the service was over, the six strangers took leave, departing through the same cleft in the wall, which closed behind them. Jalal-ud-din gave the nosegay to his wife, saying that strangers had brought it as an offering to her. The flowers were so remarkable that she sent her servant with the bouquet to the perfumers' mart of the city to ask the kind of flowers. The merchants were all astonished, never having seen such leaves. At length, however, a spice merchant from India recognized them to be the petals of a flower that grows in the south of India in Ceylon. Jalal-ud-din then told her to take the greatest care of the nosegay, as it had been sent to her by the florist of the lost earthly paradise, through Indian saints, as a special tribute.

## The Sufis, the Mystics of Persia

The teachings of the Sufis appear to have originated with the Prophet Mohammed himself. He was not only a brilliant moralist, religious leader, and statesman, but was also, by temperament, a mystic and ascetic. Throughout his life, he cultivated detachment from worldly honors and material possessions. The responsibilities of his high calling impelled him to set an example of moderate conduct, piety, and self-sacrifice. His numerous duties also demanded a well-organized life, in which concern for his faith and his people took precedent over his personal interests. We know that he was given to visions, practiced vigils, and was distinguished for humility and gentle resignation to the Will of God. Like most religious founders, he was quite different in character from those who later extended the temporal dominion of his faith.

After the death of the Prophet, Islam passed through a difficult and disputatious period. Almost immediately, the regions which had received the doctrine were involved in civil wars and came under the influence of ambitious despots and tyrants. The success of Islam produced new aristocracies which became obsessed by wealth, luxury, and power. The lines of orthodoxy were so clearly drawn as to leave the more thoughtful and sincere without any religious instruction suitable to their needs. As the faith increased in temporal wealth and honor, it catered to the selfishness and arrogance of privileged classes, and departed dramatically from the simple example and code of the prophet. There is an almost exact parallel between the rise of Moslem and Christian mysticism. Many of the austere practices of both faiths resulted from a revulsion against the corruption in the social systems of the times. The Orders of Flagellants which developed in Italy, and spread over the greater part of Europe during the Medieval period, revealed the operations of the collective conscience of society.

The Sufis belonged originally to that system of religious mysticism which is called *Quietism*. The Quietist seeks escape from the exigencies of living by retiring into himself, detaching his mind and emotions from all worldly entanglements, and directing the forces of his consciousness toward a participation in the Divine love and understanding. Many Quietist groups have excellent reputations for good works and have made practical contributions to the advancement of society. They are in the world but not of it. They usually choose noncompetitive trades and professions, and decline to cooperate with destructive policies. Their attitudes, being contrary to the approved policies of their time, are frequently misunderstood by their neighbors. The members, therefore, must endure afflictions and humiliations, and demonstrate their integrity by accepting patiently and kindly the indignities that are heaped upon them. The world has not yet learned that it takes a truly strong person to practice patience and humility. Quietists may form themselves into groups or sects, or they may remain members of prevailing religious Orders. In most cases, they can derive authority from the lives of great prophets and saints, whose examples are admired but not practiced by the orthodox.

The Sufis originally sought to find the spiritual consolation which they believed to be the essence of the Moslem doctrine. They were distinguished merely by the steadfastness with which they held to the spirit of the revelation. They declined to become involved in the luxuriousness of their contemporaries, and were ridiculed for their failure to share in the prosperous but unethical policies of their neighbors. Quietism, however, leads almost inevitably to religious experiences beyond mere piety and patience. The mind compensates the Quietist by opening to him an internal life that impels toward mysticism. Although, in the beginning, the search is primarily for peace, tranquility itself brings inevitable refinement of the psychic organism.

Those who have shared in mystical exaltations naturally desire to instruct others. The circumstances which lead the mystic to the enlargement of his inner vision soon become the disciplines of his followers. Quietism is often associated with repentance. Those least sinful are most burdened by their vices. The hearty sinner seldom repents. Mystical revelations usually burden the soul with the memories of earlier guilt. The years which preceded the awakening become a heavy burden on the conscience until, like good St. Augustine, the convert feels himself required to spend his remaining years expiating the delinquencies of his youth. It requires more illumination than even most mystics attain to rise above the guilt mechanisms of the mind. Even the recognition of the eternal love and understanding of God is not strong enough to prevent the repentant sinner from striving desperately for a salvation which seems almost inaccessible even to the penitent.

To the Sufis, their mystical convictions are timeless and ageless and entirely outside the limitations of history. They do not regard themselves as descending from a particular prophet or teacher, but rather as the preservers and unfolders of eternal truth. Several streams of mystical convictions mingled in the descent of Sufistic metaphysics. The sect was strongly influenced by Christian hermits, who retired from the busy cosmopolitan communities to cultivate their spiritual convictions in remote places. Mohammed himself contacted such recluses, and received from them a favorable impression of the original teachings of Jesus. This impression became an integral part of Moslem mysticism. The Sufis were also affected by an influx of Buddhism from Central Asia.\* The serenity and internal richness of the Buddhist life-way appealed strongly to these separatists, and was in dramatic contrast to the arrogance and worldliness of the Caliphate.

A third and no less significant source of inspiration was Alexandrian Neoplatonism, which was introduced along with other elements of classical thinking when the Moslem world became immersed in Greek philosophy.† It might not

---

\* See J. G. R. Forlong, *Faiths of Man, A Cyclopaedia of Religions*.
† See *The Mystics of Islam* by Reynold A. Nicholson.

be amiss to suggest that Sufism is in many respects Islamic Neoplatonism. From the Alexandrian mystics, the Sufis inherited the consciousness of religious unity, and the advancement of human consciousness, by degrees or stages, from complete materialism to absolute idealism. It is believed that the Sufis contributed a powerful spiritual incentive to the Dervish Orders, greatly refining and beautifying these sects.

Albert Mackey contemplates the possible connection between Sufi mysticism and European Freemasonry: ". . . We may well be surprised at the coincidences existing between the customs and the dogmas of the Sofis [sic], and we would naturally be curious to investigate the causes of the close communication which existed at various times during the Crusades between the Mohammedan sect of philosophers and the Christian Order of Templars." He strengthens his argument by quoting *The Gnostics and Their Remains* by C. W. King, *Anacalypsis* by Godfrey Higgins, and the work of Sir William Jones in his *Asiatic Researches*.*

Gradually, the Sufis developed a kind of symbolical language with which they clothed their principal tenets. They bestowed new and subtle meanings, known only to themselves, upon common and familiar terms, in order that they might share their spiritual experiences with others of similar convictions. Like the Troubadours, they composed songs and poems apparently amorous and even sensual, and conveyed the impression to the uninitiated that they were devoted to the gratification of the passions and appetites. According to C. W. King, "Arabian influence brightly manifests itself in the poetry of the Troubadours, half-amatory, half-mystical like its model, of a spirit differing as widely from the materialism of classic elegiacs, as does the pointed 'Saracenic' architecture, with all its forms suggested by the tent-pole and curtain, from the massive Romanesque which it so rapidly displaced."†

---

\* See *An Encyclopedia of Freemasonry.*
† *The Gnostics and Their Remains.*

The *Quatrains of Omar Khayyam* seem to suggest that the celebrated tentmaker was a disillusioned man who found his greater comfort in "a jug of wine, a book of verse, and thou." The "vocabulary of love and wine," as it has been called, was adopted for the same protective reasons that produced the fantastic terminology of the alchemists. The Sufis were drifting further and further from the orthodoxy of Islam, or it might be better to say that Islam was drifting away from the simple and devout example of its founder. The position of the Sufis was hazarded by the enlargement of their own vision. No longer bound by the strict orthodoxy of the Moslem world, the Sufis found it expedient to appear to be dedicated to nothing more significant than pleasure slightly shadowed by the realization of inevitable dissolution.

Some derive the word *Sufi* from a root meaning *wool;* others think it to be identical with *sophia,* or *wisdom.*\* As in the case of minstrels and trouveres, the fair and pure "beloved" was no mortal woman, but truth itself, which these mystics longed after with all the ardor of love-sick swains. Like the dark maiden of Solomon's Song, who was indeed the Black Virgin of Ephesus, and Beatrice, the beloved of Dante, the unattainable mistress of the Sufis was divine wisdom—the Virgin of the World. The Sufis' cup of wine was the chalice of ecstasy, the wine of life, the very power of God which intoxicated the soul, depriving the mind of reason, and delivering the enraptured saint from the burden of worldliness. The fatalism of the Sufis was a statement of complete emancipation from materialism and all its consequences. Life ends in silence; ambitions end in darkness; possessions rot away; and that which remains is reality, that inevitable fact of union with a Divine reality which is beyond knowing or definition.

Those who accepted literally the concept of mystical nihilism, considered the doctrines as the ultimate form of philosophical pessimism. To borrow a term from the desert,

---

\* See *Encyclopedia of Religion and Ethics.*

"it was all thunder without rain." The empty cup was broken at the well. Man came forth as a flower and was cut down, and poets chanted sadly the futility of existence. Even today, the *Rubaiyat* creates a nostalgic mood, catering to the human instinct to lament over everything in general and nothing in particular. We are most happy when a little sad, and we are most comfortable when we comfort ourselves. To the orthodox, the Sufi is gentle, but a little mad. He rejects heaven and hell and the earthly region which lies between. He lives in space, nourished by his love and wine.

Sufism divides the initiated teachers of mankind into three groups or classes, and accepts them as the illumined guardians and guides of human destiny. These heaven-sent ones are Masters, Prophets, and Saints. All aspiring mortals verge toward inclusion in one of these groups, and as they advance along the stations of the Sufistic Mysteries, they receive appropriate internal inspiration, which they manifest through works of godliness.* The Masters are those who are called the warlike teachers. They are the army of the enlightened, which must struggle against the forces of darkness. They fight the good fight, overcoming evil with the sharp, bright sword of truth. It is their destiny to become the spiritual governors and leaders of the race, and from them is chosen the governing body of the future. The Saints are the consolers, the peacemakers, the gentle ones who bring the message of love. They strive only by the example of humility. They are the servants of Allah, and they travel as the heart dictates. They bring the medicine which heals the sickness of souls, and they sing the song of the Beloved. They are the eternal priesthood, and the love of God flows through them as living waters changed by a miracle into wine.

Between the Master and the Saint stands the Prophet, the keeper of the middle road. In him the extremes find

---

*For an analysis of the "stations" in Sufi theory, see A. J. Arberry's *Sufism*.

common ground. He is the teacher; he reveals the doctrine; he is the messenger of the Divine Will. Through him the purposes of God are revealed. The Prophet is the enlightened educator, and he teaches through both wisdom and experience. The Prophets point the way to the perfection of arts and sciences. They protect the program for universal enlightenment, and in the end they form the Eternal University, the College of the Works. They reveal that all knowledge is truth in part, and that the ways of learning end in the internal understanding which is the apperception of the fullness of the Divine mind. The three Orders are, therefore, the warriors, the priests, and the teachers of righteousness, and each human being, according to the instincts of his own soul finds one of these paths opening within himself, and selects that which is the fulfillment of his own innermost resolution.

The modern trend in Sufi mysticism is away from all formalization of devotional practices. Theirs is a part of rest after labor. There is no place in their doctrine for a conflict of creeds or clash of opinions. They never argue about their beliefs or try to convert or influence those of other religious convictions. They seek rather to reveal Sufism as a quality of devotion which may be practiced by all who love God and seek to serve their fellow men. They have no special message for the intellectual except to relax and experience the love of God. They feel that this experience of the omnipresence of the Divine is the solution to the dissensions of mankind. Nothing can be proved by disputation; nothing can be solved by conversion. Truth can neither be defended nor assailed. Those who experience the presence of God require no other demonstration of the wonder of life. Sufism opens the door for those who are weary and heavy-laden, and therefore holds a peculiar fascination for that minority of troubled mortals which has found no consolation in material accomplishment.

The sect practices, in a modified form, those Eastern disciplines which strengthen the contemplative life. The Sufis do not recommend a solitary existence, but rather the practice of internal peace without neglect of natural responsibilities. They have formed monastic houses and places of retreat, but these are symbolical and are reserved for those inclined by their own internal requirements to seek solitude. Recently, some Sufistic groups have gained considerable distinction for their studies in comparative religion and for their industrious efforts to unite Near Eastern sects in the communion of spiritual brotherhood. They are not aggressive, and are dominated by a sincere belief that those who have reached the degree of understanding which requires a larger internal life will be drawn naturally to the mystical life of illumination, under one name or another.

# Works on Occult Philosophy by Manly P. Hall

## ORDERS OF THE GREAT WORK: ALCHEMY
### Adepts in the Western Esoteric Tradition, Part 2

Herein is set forth the origin of alchemy, its rise in Egypt as the secret doctrine of Hermes, its migration to Arabia, and its relation to the early schools of Christianity. Through Alchemy's travels many pioneers in the field emerged, including Roger Bacon, Raymond Lully, and Nicholas Flamel. The letters of Sendivogius to the Brotherhood of the Rosy Cross, almost completely unknown to the modern world, are discussed. Illustrated.

$15.95. Paperback. 108pp. ISBN: 0-89314-534-3

## TWELVE WORLD TEACHERS

An illustrated summary of the twelve mystic and enlightened teachers who possessed the fullest measure of those intellectual virtues that sustain civilization, inspiring others to more enlightened codes of living: Akhenaten, Lao-Tse, Hermes Trismegistus, Plato, Orpheus, Jesus Christ, Zoroaster, Mohammed, Buddha, Padmasambhava, Confucius, and Quetzalcoatl..

$16.95. Paperback. 240pp. ISBN: 0-89314-816-4

## WORDS TO THE WISE:
### A Practical Guide to the Esoteric Sciences

Examines the teachings of the Mystery Schools, the five steps of self-unfoldment, and how the practice of ancient disciplines can lead to a more purposeful life. Discern the difference between true and false paths to wisdom, and what is expected of the sincere truth seeker.

$15.95. Paperback. 160pp. ISBN: 0-89314-814-8

*Visit Our Online Catalog at* www.prs.org/prspub.htm

# UNIVERSITY of PHILOSOPHICAL RESEARCH
## A CONTEMPORARY WISDOM ACADEMY

## Nationally Accredited MASTER'S DEGREES

- ### Consciousness Studies
- ### Transformational Psychology

**TRANSFORM YOUR PERSPECTIVE AND YOUR LIFE** | In today's global postmodern world, a holistic, multicultural, evolutionary and spiritual perspective is a **necessity in every life enterprise**. For those lacking these consciousness skills, today's world presents a crisis; for those possessing them, a wide opportunity and a promise. Whatever your life goals, with a graduate degree from UPR, you will be able to **maximize your potential** and be at the **leading edge of your expectations**.

**WHAT OUR GRADUATES BECOME** | Our graduates are impelled by the aspiration to become leaders of society, as teachers, writers, scholars, life-coaches and administrators.

## Online Learning | the wave of the future

- **UPR uses universally accessible online and telecommunication technologies to teach its graduate courses**
- **Learn in your free time and wherever you can access the Internet and/or a CD player**
- **Enjoy the privilege of interacting with the world's leading teachers of wisdom**
- **Online learning keeps tuition at affordable rates**

**For complete information, including a Catalog visit our website at http://www.uprs.edu**

e-mail | registrar@uprs.edu
phone | 800.548.4062
fax | 323.663.9443

**UNIVERSITY OF PHILOSOPHICAL RESEARCH**
3910 Los Feliz Boulevard, Los Angeles, CA 90027